CW01558428

DASH DIET COOKBOOK 2024 UK

1500 Days of Quick & Delicious Low-Sodium Recipes for Time-Crunched Individuals, Lower Blood Pressure, and Weight Loss Goals (28-Week Meal Plan Saves the Day!)

LIZZIE K. BAILEY

Copyright © 2024 By **LIZZIE K. BAILEY**. All rights reserved worldwide.

No part of this book may be reproduced or transmitted in any form or by any means, electronic or mechanical, including photocopying, recording, or by any information storage and retrieval system, without written permission from the publisher, except for the inclusion of brief quotations in a review.

Warning-Disclaimer:

The purpose of this book is to educate and entertain. The author or publisher does not guarantee that anyone following the techniques, suggestions, tips, ideas, or strategies will become successful. The author and publisher shall have neither liability nor responsibility to anyone with respect to any loss or damage caused, or alleged to be caused, directly or indirectly, by the information contained in this book.

This copyright notice and disclaimer apply to the entirety of the book and its contents, whether in print or electronic form, and extend to all future editions or revisions of the book. Unauthorized use or reproduction of this book or its contents is strictly prohibited and may result in legal action.

INTRODUCTION:

UNDERSTANDING THE DASH DIET

What is the Dash diet? The Dash diet, short for Dietary Approaches to Stop Hypertension, is a comprehensive and scientifically backed eating plan that focuses on consuming nutrient rich foods while reducing sodium intake. Developed by the National Institutes of Health (NIH) in the United States, the Dash diet was originally designed to help lower blood pressure. However, research has shown that it offers numerous other health benefits, including sustainable weight loss and improved overall wellbeing.

The Dash diet emphasizes the consumption of fruits, vegetables, whole grains, lean proteins, and low fat dairy products. These foods are rich in essential nutrients such as vitamins, minerals, fiber, and antioxidants, which are vital for optimal health. By prioritizing these nutrient dense options, individuals following the Dash diet can nourish their bodies and support their overall wellbeing.

In addition to its focus on wholesome foods, the Dash diet also promotes a reduction in sodium intake. Excessive sodium consumption has been linked to high blood pressure, which increases the risk of heart disease and stroke. By limiting sodium intake to no more than 2,300 milligrams per day (or 1,500 milligrams for individuals with hypertension or prehypertension), the Dash diet helps individuals achieve and maintain healthy blood pressure levels.

Unlike fad diets that restrict certain food groups or require drastic calorie reduction, the Dash diet provides a balanced approach to nutrition. It encourages the consumption of a wide variety of foods from all major food groups, ensuring individuals receive a broad spectrum of essential nutrients. This makes the Dash diet not only effective for weight loss but also sustainable for long term health maintenance.

By adopting the Dash diet, individuals can improve their overall diet quality and make lasting lifestyle changes. Whether your goal is to lose weight, reduce blood pressure, or simply embrace a natural, healthy lifestyle, the principles of the Dash diet can guide you towards success. Throughout this book, we will explore the delicious and flavorful recipes that make the Dash diet enjoyable, as well as provide you with valuable *tips* and guidance for incorporating this lifestyle into your daily routine. Get ready to revolutionize your health and embark on a journey towards optimal wellbeing with the Dash diet!

The scientific evidence

Scientific evidence has consistently shown the effectiveness of the Dash diet in promoting weight loss and improving overall health. Numerous studies have demonstrated that following the Dash diet can lead to lower blood pressure levels, reduce the risk of cardiovascular diseases, and support sustainable weight loss.

One study published in the New England Journal of Medicine found that individuals who followed the Dash diet experienced a significant reduction in blood pressure, particularly for those with hypertension. Another study, conducted by researchers at Johns Hopkins University, showed that adhering to the Dash diet resulted in lower cholesterol levels and improved heart health.

Furthermore, research has indicated that the Dash diet can contribute to long term weight loss success. A study published in the Annals of Internal Medicine found that participants who followed the Dash diet for eight weeks experienced significant weight loss compared to those on a standard American diet. The sustained weight loss observed in the study suggests that the Dash diet is a viable approach for individuals looking to achieve and maintain a healthy weight.

It is important to note that while weight loss is a desirable outcome for many individuals, it is not the only benefit associated with following the Dash diet. In addition to supporting weight management, the Dash diet has been shown to reduce the risk of chronic diseases such as diabetes and promote overall wellbeing.

By incorporating nutrient rich foods, reducing sodium intake, and adopting a balanced approach to nutrition, individuals can harness the power of the Dash diet to improve their health outcomes. This book will provide you with all the tools and information you need to embrace this transformative lifestyle and achieve your weight loss and wellness goals.

Comparison with other popular diets

When looking at popular diets such as the Mediterranean diet or ketogenic diet, it's important to understand how the Dash diet stands out as a more sustainable lifestyle choice. While each diet may have its merits and benefits, the Dash diet provides a balanced approach to nutrition that is both realistic and achievable in the long term.

One key difference between the Dash diet and other popular diets is its focus on overall health and wellbeing, rather than solely on weight loss. While weight loss can certainly be a goal of the Dash diet, it prioritizes nourishing the body with nutrient rich foods and reducing sodium intake to promote heart health, lower blood pressure, and reduce the risk of chronic diseases such as diabetes and cardiovascular disease.

Unlike the restrictive nature of some diets that eliminate entire food groups or severely restrict calorie intake, the Dash diet encourages individuals to consume a wide variety of foods from all food groups. This inclusivity allows for greater flexibility and enjoyment in meal planning, making it easier to sustain this lifestyle over time. By emphasizing whole grains, lean proteins, fruits, vegetables, and low fat dairy products, the Dash diet provides a balanced nutritional profile that supports overall health and wellness.

Additionally, the Dash diet promotes mindful eating and portion control rather than strict calorie counting. This approach allows individuals to listen to their bodies' hunger and fullness cues, fostering a healthier relationship with food and promoting a sustainable approach to eating.

Overall, the Dash diet offers a comprehensive and holistic approach to healthy living and weight loss. It takes into account not only the nutritional aspects of food but also promotes positive lifestyle changes that can be maintained for years to come. By incorporating nutrient rich foods, reducing sodium intake, and embracing a balanced approach to nutrition, individuals can achieve their health goals while enjoying delicious meals that nourish both body and soul.

BENEFITS BEYOND WEIGHT LOSS

Following the Dash diet offers numerous advantages beyond just weight loss. Incorporating this eating plan into your lifestyle can lead to improved overall health and a reduced risk of chronic diseases such as diabetes and cardiovascular disease. By focusing on nutrient rich foods and reducing sodium intake, the Dash diet promotes long term wellbeing.

1. **Improved heart health:** The Dash diet has been shown to lower blood pressure, a major risk factor for heart disease. By prioritizing fruits, vegetables, whole grains, and lean proteins while minimizing processed foods and high sodium INGREDIENTS, you can support cardiovascular health and reduce the likelihood of developing heart related complications.

2. **Reduced risk of diabetes:** The Dash diet's emphasis on balanced meals and controlled portion sizes can help regulate blood sugar levels, making it an effective approach for managing or preventing diabetes. By selecting complex carbohydrates, lean proteins, and healthy fats, you can maintain stable blood glucose levels and reduce the risk of insulin resistance.

3. **Enhanced nutrient intake:** The diverse array of foods encouraged in the Dash diet ensures that you receive a wide range of essential nutrients. From vitamins and minerals to antioxidants and fiber, a well rounded diet supports optimal bodily functions, boosts the immune system, and helps prevent nutrient deficiencies.

4. **Increased energy levels:** By nourishing your body with wholesome foods and avoiding energy draining processed snacks and sugary beverages, you can experience sustained energy throughout the day. The Dash diet provides a balance of macronutrients that fuels your body efficiently, helping you feel more energized and focused.

5. **Improved digestive health:** The fiber rich nature of many Dash diet foods promotes healthy digestion by supporting regular bowel movements, preventing constipation, and fostering a diverse gut microbiome. Incorporating plenty of fruits, vegetables, whole grains, and legumes into your meals provides the necessary fiber to maintain optimal digestive function.

6. **Enhanced satiety and reduced cravings:** The Dash diet focuses on nutrient dense foods that are filling and satisfying, which can help curb cravings and prevent overeating. By including lean proteins, whole grains, and healthy fats in your meals, you can stay full for longer periods and reduce the temptation to indulge in unhealthy snacks.

7. **Long term sustainability:** Unlike many other fad diets, the Dash diet is a sustainable lifestyle choice that can be followed for the long term. It promotes a balanced approach to eating, allowing for flexibility while still prioritizing nutritious foods. This makes it easier to adopt as a permanent way of life, ensuring continued health benefits well into the future.

By embracing the Dash diet and incorporating its principles into your everyday life, you can enjoy a multitude of benefits beyond weight loss alone. Improved heart health, reduced risk of chronic diseases, enhanced nutrient intake, increased energy levels, improved digestive health, enhanced satiety, and long term sustainability are just some of the rewards that await those who choose to follow this natural and healthy eating plan.

The impact of high sodium intake on blood pressure and overall health

Incorporating the Dash diet into daily life can seem overwhelming at first, but with a few practical *tips* and strategies, it can become a seamless part of your routine. This section will guide you on how to create a grocery shopping list, meal plan, and adapt recipes to align with Dash diet principles. Additionally, it will provide valuable information on how to navigate dining out and social settings while following the Dash diet.

When it comes to grocery shopping, it's important to focus on whole, unprocessed foods that are low in sodium. Start by making a list of fruits, vegetables, whole grains, lean proteins, and low fat dairy products. Plan your meals around these nutritious INGREDIENTS, and avoid purchasing items high in added sugars or unhealthy fats. Be sure to read food labels carefully to check for hidden sources of sodium.

To make meal planning easier, try dedicating a specific day each week for planning and prepping your meals. Look for recipes that align with Dash diet principles and create a schedule for breakfast, lunch, dinner, and snacks. Having a meal plan in place will not only save you time and stress but also help you stay on track with your healthy eating goals. Consider batch cooking certain dishes like soups or casseroles that can be portioned out and enjoyed throughout the week.

Adapting recipes to fit the Dash diet can be simple with a few substitutions. For example, replace salt with herbs and spices to enhance flavor without adding sodium. Choose low sodium or no added salt versions of canned **INGREDIENTS** like beans or tomatoes. Experiment with different cooking methods such as grilling or steaming instead of frying. With a little creativity, you can still enjoy delicious meals while adhering to the Dash diet.

When dining out, it's essential to be mindful of your choices. Check the menu ahead of time if possible and look for options that include plenty of vegetables, lean proteins, and whole grains. Ask for dressings and sauces on the side to control the amount of sodium added to your meal. It's also helpful to let the server know about any dietary restrictions or preferences, as they may be able to accommodate your needs.

In social settings, it can be challenging to stick to your healthy eating plan, but it's not impossible. Be proactive by bringing a dish or snack that aligns with the Dash diet to share with others. This ensures there will be at least one healthy option available. Additionally, practice portion control and mindful eating by listening to your body's hunger and fullness cues. Don't feel pressured to overeat just because others are indulging.

By incorporating these practical *tips* and strategies into your daily life, you can successfully adopt the Dash diet and make healthier choices for long term wellbeing. Remember, it's a journey, and small steps can lead to significant changes over time. Embrace the Dash diet as a sustainable lifestyle choice and enjoy the benefits it brings to your health and overall quality of life.

The Benefits of Reducing Sodium Intake

Reducing Sodium Intake and its Impact on Blood Pressure and Overall Health

Excessive sodium consumption has been linked to various health issues, most notably high blood pressure. When we consume too much sodium, our bodies retain water to dilute the excess salt in our bloodstream. This increased water volume puts a strain on our blood vessels and can lead to elevated blood pressure levels.

High blood pressure, or hypertension, is a major risk factor for heart disease, stroke, and kidney disease. It is often referred to as the "silent killer" because it typically doesn't cause any noticeable symptoms until it reaches a dangerous level. That's why it is crucial to be proactive in reducing sodium intake and maintaining a healthy blood pressure.

The recommended daily sodium intake for adults is less than 2,300 milligrams (mg), which is about one teaspoon of salt. However, most people exceed this limit due to the high sodium content in processed foods, restaurant meals, and fast food.

By reducing sodium intake, individuals can lower their blood pressure and improve their overall health. Studies have shown that even a small reduction in sodium intake can have significant health benefits. For example, a systematic review and meta analysis published in The Cochrane Database of Systematic Reviews found that reducing sodium intake resulted in a modest reduction in blood pressure across all age groups. This reduction was seen in both individuals with normal blood pressure and those with hypertension.

In addition to its impact on blood pressure, excessive sodium consumption can also contribute to bloating and water retention. This can make individuals feel uncomfortable and affect their body weight. By cutting back on sodium, individuals may experience a decrease in water retention and bloating, leading to improved body composition and potential weight loss.

It is important to note that reducing sodium intake alone may not be sufficient for managing high blood pressure or improving overall health. A comprehensive approach that includes regular physical activity, stress management, and a balanced diet rich in fruits, vegetables, whole grains, and lean proteins is essential.

By understanding the impact of high sodium intake on blood pressure and overall health, individuals can take proactive steps to reduce their sodium consumption and embrace a healthier lifestyle. Making conscious choices to limit processed foods and restaurant meals while increasing the consumption of whole, unprocessed foods will not only support blood pressure management but also contribute to improved overall wellbeing.

The Correlation Between Reduced Sodium Intake And Weight Loss:

Did you know that reducing your sodium intake can contribute to weight loss? It may seem counterintuitive, but studies have shown a strong link between reduced sodium consumption and shedding those extra pounds.

One of the main reasons for this connection is the way sodium affects water retention in the body. When we consume high amounts of sodium, our bodies hold onto excess water, leading to bloating and a temporary increase in weight. By reducing our sodium intake, we can help regulate the body's water balance, reducing bloating and the associated temporary weight gain.

Additionally, excessive sodium intake has been linked to higher levels of leptin, a hormone responsible for regulating appetite and storing fat. When we consume too much sodium, it can disrupt leptin signaling, leading to increased feelings of hunger and potentially overeating. By reducing sodium intake, we can help restore proper appetite regulation and support healthy eating habits.

It's important to note that the correlation between reduced sodium intake and weight loss does not imply that simply cutting back on salt will result in significant weight loss alone. Weight loss is a complex process influenced by various factors such as overall calorie intake, physical activity level, and individual metabolic differences. However, by incorporating a low sodium diet into a comprehensive weight loss plan, individuals may experience enhanced results and improved overall health.

In the following chapters, we'll delve deeper into strategies for reducing sodium in everyday meals without sacrificing flavor. We'll explore alternative herbs, spices, and natural flavor enhancers that can add depth and complexity to dishes without relying on excessive salt. Together, let's embark on this journey towards healthier living and weight loss through reduced sodium intake.

Tips And Strategies For Reducing Sodium In Everyday Meals Without Sacrificing Flavor

1. **Experiment with herbs and spices:** Instead of relying on salt to enhance the taste of your dishes, explore the wide range of herbs and spices available. Incorporate flavorful options like basil, cilantro, rosemary, cumin, turmeric, and paprika to add a burst of taste to your meals. Not only do herbs and spices provide an array of flavors, but they also offer numerous health benefits.

2. **Use natural flavor enhancers:** Opt for natural flavor enhancers to replace salt in your cooking. INGREDIENTS like garlic, onions, lemon juice, and vinegars can be excellent substitutes for adding depth and complexity to your dishes. They provide a tangy or savory punch without the excess sodium.

3. **Read food labels carefully**: Make it a habit to read food labels when shopping for groceries. This allows you to identify hidden sources of sodium in packaged foods. Be on the lookout for INGREDIENTS such as monosodium glutamate (MSG), sodium nitrate, sodium benzoate, and sodium bicarbonate. Choosing low sodium options or making your own versions of these foods can significantly reduce your sodium intake.

4. **Cook from scratch**: Preparing your meals from scratch gives you complete control over the amount of sodium you consume. By using fresh INGREDIENTS and minimizing the use of processed foods or readymade sauces, you can significantly reduce your sodium intake while enjoying flavorful and nutritious meals.

5. **Rinse canned foods**: If you choose to incorporate canned goods into your recipes, give them a thorough rinse before using them. This rinsing process can wash away excess sodium that is often present due to the preservation process.

6. **Gradually reduce sodium levels**: Aim to gradually reduce the amount of salt you use in your cooking. Your taste buds will gradually adjust to lower sodium levels over time. Start by reducing the amount used in recipes by half and gradually decrease it further until you find a level that suits your taste preferences.

By implementing these **tips** and strategies, you can effortlessly reduce your sodium intake without compromising flavor. Embracing these new cooking techniques will not only support your weight loss goals but also enhance your overall health and wellbeing.

Sodium reduction in specific food categories

One of the key steps to reducing sodium intake is to identify and replace high sodium foods in your diet. In this section, we will break down common high sodium food categories and provide recommendations for healthier alternatives and homemade versions.

1. Processed Meats:

Processed meats like bacon, sausages, deli meats, and hot dogs are often loaded with sodium as a preservative. Opt for fresh lean meats such as chicken breast, turkey, or fish. You can also try making your own deli style meats by roasting or grilling them at home and slicing them thinly for sandwiches.

2. Canned Soups and Broths:

Canned soups and broths are convenient but can contain staggering amounts of sodium. Look for low sodium or sodium free options, or better yet, make your own homemade soups and broths using fresh vegetables, herbs, and spices. This way, you have more control over the amount of sodium in your meals.

3. Fast Food:

Fast food is notorious for its high sodium content. When craving burgers or fries, consider making healthier versions at home using lean ground beef or turkey, whole grain buns, and baking instead of frying the potatoes. This way, you can enjoy the flavors you love while reducing the sodium levels.

4. Condiments and Sauces:

Condiments like ketchup, soy sauce, salad dressings, and barbecue sauce can add a significant amount of sodium to your meals. Opt for reduced sodium or low sodium versions of these condiments, or try making your own sauces using fresh **INGREDIENTS** and spices. You'll be surprised at how flavorful homemade condiments can be.

5. Snack Foods:

Snack foods like chips, pretzels, popcorn, and salted nuts are often high in sodium. Look for low sodium or unsalted versions, or try making your own healthy snacks at home. Air popped popcorn, roasted chickpeas, or homemade kale chips are delicious alternatives that satisfy cravings without the excessive sodium.

By being aware of high sodium food categories and making smart choices, you can significantly reduce your sodium intake while still enjoying flavorful meals. Experiment with homemade versions of your favorite dishes and explore different seasonings to enhance taste without relying on salt. Your taste buds and your health will thank you!

Implementing a low sodium diet for improved health can be achieved through practical steps that gradually reduce sodium intake and provide guidance on meal planning and grocery shopping. It is essential to approach this transition with patience and commitment to long term success.

1. Gradually reduce sodium intake:

- Start by slowly reducing the amount of salt used in cooking and at the table. Experiment with herbs, spices, and natural flavor enhancers to add taste without relying on sodium.
- Gradually decrease the consumption of processed foods and restaurant meals, which are often high in sodium. Replace them with homemade meals using fresh, whole **INGREDIENTS**.
- Be mindful of hidden sources of sodium, such as condiments, sauces, and prepackaged foods. Read food labels carefully to identify products that are low in sodium or have no added salt.

2. Plan and prepare low sodium meals:

- Create a meal plan that focuses on whole foods, including fruits, vegetables, lean proteins, and whole grains. These provide essential nutrients while naturally being low in sodium.
- Cook meals from scratch whenever possible to have full control over the amount of sodium added. Use fresh or dried herbs and spices to enhance flavor instead of relying on salt.

- Incorporate a variety of cooking methods, like baking, grilling, steaming, or sautéing, to bring out the natural flavors of **INGREDIENTS** without adding excessive sodium.

3. Shop smart for low sodium options:

- Build a shopping list based on low sodium ingredients, such as fresh produce, lean proteins, whole grains, and unsalted nuts.
- Select canned goods marked as low sodium or noadded salt versions. Rinse canned vegetables and legumes under cold water before using to remove excess sodium.
- Avoid purchasing heavily processed foods that are typically high in sodium. Opt for fresh alternatives whenever possible.

By implementing these strategies and gradually adopting a low sodium diet, individuals can improve their overall health and reduce the risks associated with high blood pressure. The transition may require some adjustment, but the long term benefits to wellbeing are well worth the effort.

DASH DIET
AIR FRYER
Cookbook

SCAN TO DOWNLOAD

GETTING STARTED WITH THE DASH DIET:

TIPS FOR SUCCESS

Understanding the Dash Diet Principles

The Dash diet, which stands for Dietary Approaches to Stop Hypertension, is a scientifically proven eating plan designed to lower blood pressure and promote overall health. It emphasizes consuming a wide variety of fruits, vegetables, whole grains, lean proteins, and low fat dairy products while limiting intake of sodium, saturated fats, and added sugars.

One of the main principles of the Dash diet is a focus on fruits and vegetables. These nutrient dense foods are packed with vitamins, minerals, and antioxidants that support optimal health. Aim to include a variety of colorful fruits and vegetables in your meals and snacks to ensure you're getting a wide range of beneficial nutrients.

Whole grains are another essential component of the Dash diet. They provide important fiber, vitamins, and minerals while helping to maintain steady energy levels throughout the day. Opt for whole wheat bread, brown rice, quinoa, and oatmeal instead of refined grains like white bread or white rice.

Lean proteins play a crucial role in the Dash diet as well. Choose lean cuts of meat such as skinless poultry or fish like salmon or tuna. Legumes, such as lentils and chickpeas, are also excellent sources of protein and can be used as alternatives to animal based proteins.

In addition to these food groups, the Dash diet encourages consumption of low fat dairy products like yogurt and skim milk. These dairy options provide essential nutrients such as calcium and vitamin D without adding excessive saturated fat to your diet.

Reducing sodium intake is a key aspect of the Dash diet. High sodium consumption has been linked to increased blood pressure levels and cardiovascular disease risk. To limit your sodium intake, choose fresh foods over processed ones, read food labels carefully, and season your meals with herbs and spices rather than salt.

To successfully adopt the Dash diet into your daily routine, it's important to gradually incorporate its principles into your meals and snacks. Start by making small changes, such as swapping out high sodium condiments for lower sodium options or adding an extra serving of vegetables to your plate. Over time, these small adjustments will become habits that contribute to a healthier lifestyle.

By understanding the key principles and guidelines of the Dash diet, you can begin to make informed choices about the foods you consume. The emphasis on nutrient dense **INGREDIENTS**, reduced sodium intake, and gradual changes sets the foundation for a successful transition to a Dash diet lifestyle.

Practical Advice for Transitioning to a Dash Diet Lifestyle:

Transitioning to the Dash diet and embracing a healthier lifestyle can be both exciting and challenging. However, with the right mindset and practical strategies, individuals can successfully make sustainable changes to their eating habits. Here are some practical *tips* for transitioning to a Dash diet lifestyle:

Make Gradual Changes: Instead of completely overhauling your diet overnight, aim to make small, gradual changes. Start by incorporating more fruits and vegetables into your meals, replacing processed snacks with healthier options, and gradually reducing your sodium intake. This approach allows you to adjust to new flavors and helps ensure long term success.

Set Realistic Goals: It's important to set realistic goals when starting any new diet or lifestyle change. Focus on achievable targets such as incorporating one additional serving of vegetables into your meals each day or reducing your sodium intake by a certain percentage each week. Celebrate each milestone reached, no matter how small, as it will keep you motivated and moving forward.

Create a Supportive Environment: Surround yourself with people who support your decision to follow the Dash diet. Share your goals with friends and family so they can offer encouragement and understanding. If possible, find a buddy who is also interested in following the diet, as you can provide mutual support and motivation.

Plan Ahead: Planning ahead is crucial for success on the Dash diet. Take time each week to plan your meals and create a shopping list based on the Dash diet principles. This will help you stay organized, save time, and ensure that you have nutritious ingredients on hand. Consider prepping meals in advance or batch cooking to make healthy eating more convenient during busy days.

Keep a Food Journal: Keeping a food journal can provide valuable insights into your eating habits and help you identify areas for improvement. Record what you eat, portion sizes, and any emotions or triggers associated with eating. Reviewing your journal regularly can help you make more informed choices and identify patterns that may hinder your progress.

Overcome Challenges: Be prepared for challenges along your Dash diet journey. For instance, you may encounter cravings for high sodium foods or face social situations where it's difficult to make Dash friendly choices. To overcome these challenges, have a plan in place. Find healthier alternatives to your favorite high sodium snacks, have nutritious options readily available when dining out, and develop strategies to cope with emotional eating.

Stay Motivated: Maintaining motivation is key to long term success on the Dash diet. Surround yourself with positive reminders of why you embarked on this journey, such as inspirational quotes or hereinafter pictures. Celebrate milestones, whether it's pounds lost or inches reduced, and reward yourself with nonfood treats like a massage or a new workout outfit.

Remember, transitioning to a Dash diet lifestyle is a process that takes time and patience. Focus on the progress you make rather than perfection. By incorporating these practical *tips* into your daily life, you'll be well on your way to embracing a successful Dash diet lifestyle and achieving your health and weight loss goals.

Meal Planning and Grocery Shopping *Tips*:

Creating a meal plan that aligns with the Dash diet is an essential step in successfully adopting this healthy lifestyle. By planning ahead, you can ensure that your meals are nutritious, flavorful, and low in sodium. Here are some practical *tips* to help you create a Dash diet meal plan that fits your individual preferences and dietary needs:

Set Realistic Goals: Before creating your meal plan, consider your lifestyle, schedule, and personal food preferences. Set realistic goals for yourself, keeping in mind that gradual changes are more sustainable than drastic ones. Start by incorporating one or two Dash friendly meals each day and gradually increase as you become more comfortable.

Choose Nutritious Recipes: Look for recipes that incorporate a variety of fresh fruits, vegetables, whole grains, lean proteins, and low fat dairy products. Aim for a balance of nutrients in each meal to ensure you're getting all the essential vitamins and minerals your body needs.

Plan Meals in Advance: Take some time each week to plan your meals in advance. Consider your schedule, work commitments, and any events or social gatherings where you may need to modify your diet. This will help you stay organized and avoid lastminute unhealthy food choices.

Shop with a List: Before heading to the grocery store, make a list of all the INGREDIENTS you'll need for your planned meals. Stick to this list as much as possible to avoid impulse purchases of high sodium or unhealthy foods. By having a clear plan, you'll save time and be less likely to deviate from your healthy eating goals.

Read Food Labels: When shopping for packaged foods, carefully read the nutrition labels to check for sodium content. Look for items labeled "low sodium" or "no added salt." Avoid processed foods that tend to be high in sodium, such as canned soups, deli meats, and snack foods.

Stock Your Pantry: Keep your pantry well stocked with essential INGREDIENTS for easy Dash diet meal preparation. Some pantry staples to have on hand include whole grains like quinoa and brown rice, canned beans and lentils, low sodium broths, herbs and spices for flavoring, olive oil for cooking, and a variety of nuts and seeds for snacking.

Shop the Perimeter: When navigating the grocery store, focus on shopping the perimeter where you'll find fresh produce, lean meats, dairy products, and whole grains. The inner aisles tend to house processed foods that are often high in sodium and should be avoided or kept to a minimum.

Buy Fresh Produce in Season: Opt for fresh fruits and vegetables that are in season as they tend to be more flavorful, affordable, and packed with nutrients. This will also add variety to your meals throughout the year.

Consider Frozen and Canned Options: If fresh produce is not readily available or too expensive, consider using frozen or canned options. These can be just as nutritious and often more convenient. Look for frozen fruits and vegetables without added sauces or seasonings and choose low sodium canned goods whenever possible.

Prep Ahead: Once you've returned from the grocery store, take some time to prep your INGREDIENTS in advance. Chop vegetables, portion out snacks, and cook grains and proteins ahead of time. This will save you time during busy weekdays and make it easier to stick to your meal plan.

By following these meal planning and grocery shopping *tips*, you'll be well prepared to begin your Dash diet journey with confidence. With a well-thought-out meal plan and a stocked pantry, you'll have all the tools you need to succeed in embracing a healthier lifestyle focused on nourishing, flavorful meals.

Dining Out on the Dash Diet

When following the Dash diet, dining out can present challenges in sticking to the recommended guidelines. However, with some knowledge and preparation, it is still possible to make healthier choices while enjoying meals at restaurants or social events. Here are some *tips* and strategies for dining out on the Dash diet:

1. Do Your Research:

Before heading out to a restaurant, take some time to research the menu options online. Many restaurants now provide their menus on their websites, allowing you to review them in advance. Look for dishes that include lean proteins, vegetables, and whole grains. Avoid menu items that are likely to be high in sodium, such as those described as fried, breaded, or creamy.

2. Be Mindful of Preparation Methods:

Different cooking methods can have a significant impact on the overall healthfulness of a dish. Opt for grilled, baked, steamed, or broiled dishes instead of fried or sautéed options. These cooking methods often require less added fats and oils, reducing the overall calorie and sodium content of the meal.

3. Request Modifications:

Don't be afraid to ask for modifications to menu items to reduce sodium content or make them more Dash diet friendly. Ask for dressings, sauces, or gravies on the side so that you can control how much is added to your meal. Request to have your food prepared with less salt or without added salt altogether. Most restaurants are willing to accommodate special requests, especially when it comes to dietary restrictions or health concerns.

4. Choose Healthier Menu Options:

Look for menu items that incorporate plenty of fruits and vegetables. Salads with lean proteins like grilled chicken or shrimp can be excellent choices. Opt for whole grain options like whole wheat pasta or brown rice instead of refined grains. When choosing protein sources, opt for fish, lean poultry, or legumes instead of higher fat meats like beef or pork.

5. Be Mindful of Portion Sizes:

Restaurant portions tend to be larger than what we typically eat at home. To maintain a healthy calorie intake, consider sharing an entree with a dining partner or request a togo box at the beginning of the meal and set aside half of your meal for later. This can help prevent overeating and allow you to enjoy the meal without feeling deprived.

6. Choose Healthier Side Dishes:

Many restaurants offer a variety of side dishes to accompany main courses. Instead of opting for fries or other fried options, choose sides like steamed vegetables, grilled asparagus, or a side salad. If there are healthier options available, don't hesitate to make substitutions.

7. Practice Portion Control with Appetizers and Desserts:

When it comes to appetizers and desserts, it's easy to get carried away with indulgent choices. Instead of ordering high calorie or high sodium appetizers, opt for a broth based soup or a mixed green salad as a starter. For dessert, consider sharing a sweet treat with others at the table or choosing a fruit based option.

Remember that while dining out provides an opportunity to enjoy delicious food in a social setting, it's essential to make mindful choices that align with your goals on the Dash diet. By being aware of ingredient choices, preparation methods, and portion sizes, you can navigate restaurant menus with confidence and still make progress towards your health and weight loss goals.

Overcoming Common Challenges

Embarking on any new diet or lifestyle change can come with its fair share of challenges. However, by being aware of these obstacles and having a plan in place, you can overcome them and stay on track with your Dash diet journey. In this section, we will identify some common challenges faced by individuals adopting the Dash diet and provide strategies for successfully navigating them.

One challenge that many people encounter is managing cravings. As you transition to a diet that is lower in sodium and focuses on whole, unprocessed foods, you may find yourself missing certain flavors or reaching for familiar comfort foods. It's important to remember that cravings are normal and not a sign of weakness. Instead of giving in to unhealthy choices, try the following strategies:

Understand the root cause: Cravings can be triggered by emotions, stress, or even boredom. Take a moment to reflect on what might be causing your craving and find alternative ways to address those feelings. For example, if you're feeling stressed, try going for a walk or practicing deep breathing exercises instead of turning to food.

Distract yourself: Engage in an activity that takes your mind off the craving. This could be reading a book, calling a friend, or pursuing a hobby you enjoy. Many times, cravings pass if you give yourself time and space to focus on something else.

Choose healthier alternatives: If you're craving something salty, reach for a handful of unsalted nuts or make your own low sodium popcorn. If it's something sweet you're after, try indulging in a piece of fruit or a small serving of dark chocolate.

Another challenge that individuals often face when following the Dash diet is emotional eating. It's common to turn to food as a source of comfort or reward during times of stress or sadness. However, emotional eating can hinder your progress towards weight loss and overall health goals. Here are some strategies to help you deal with emotional eating:

Recognize triggers: Identify the situations or emotions that tend to lead to emotional eating. By becoming aware of your triggers, you can develop alternative coping mechanisms to address these feelings.

Find healthy outlets for emotions: Instead of turning to food, find other ways to manage your emotions. This could be engaging in physical activity, talking to a friend or therapist, writing in a journal, or practicing relaxation techniques like yoga or meditation.

Practice mindful eating: Before reaching for a snack, pause and ask yourself if you are truly hungry or if you are seeking comfort. If it's emotional hunger, try to find an alternative activity that addresses the underlying emotion.

Finally, staying consistent and maintaining progress on the Dash diet journey can sometimes be challenging. However, with the right strategies in place, you can increase your chances of long term success. Here are some *tips* to help you stay on track:

Set realistic goals: Make sure your expectations align with what is achievable and sustainable for you. Setting small, attainable goals will keep you motivated and prevent feelings of overwhelm.

Celebrate victories: Take time to recognize and celebrate your achievements, whether it's losing a few pounds or consistently sticking to your meal plan. Rewarding yourself for your efforts will reinforce positive behavior and make the journey more enjoyable.

Lean on support: Surround yourself with a supportive network of friends, family, or even online communities who understand and encourage your Dash diet journey. Having someone to share your challenges and successes with can make all the difference in staying dedicated.

Remember, the Dash diet is not a short term fix but a lifelong commitment to improving your health and wellbeing. By identifying and overcoming common challenges like managing cravings, dealing with emotional eating, and staying consistent, you can successfully navigate any roadblocks that may come your way. Stay focused on your goals, be kind to yourself, and trust in the transformative power of the Dash diet.

METABOLISM BOOSTING SECRETS: ENHANCING WEIGHT LOSS WITH THE DASH DIET

Understanding Metabolism and Its Role in Weight Loss

Metabolism plays a crucial role in weight loss and overall health. It refers to the process by which your body converts food into energy. This energy is then used by your body for various functions, such as breathing, digestion, and physical activity.

Several factors influence your metabolic rate, including age, genetics, and activity level. As we age, our metabolism tends to naturally slow down, making it easier to gain weight and harder to lose it. Additionally, genetics can play a role in determining your metabolic rate. Some individuals may naturally have a faster metabolism than others.

However, while some aspects of metabolism may be beyond our control, there are steps we can take to assess and potentially increase our metabolic rate through dietary choices. One way to evaluate your metabolism is by calculating your basal metabolic rate (BMR), which is the number of calories your body needs to perform basic functions at rest.

To assess your BMR, you can use online calculators that take into account factors such as your age, gender, weight, and height. Many fitness trackers and smartwatches also have builtin tools to estimate daily calorie burn based on factors like heart rate and activity level.

In terms of increasing metabolic rate through dietary choices, there are several strategies to consider. One important factor is ensuring you consume an adequate amount of calories each day. Severely restricting calorie intake can actually lower your metabolic rate as your body goes into "starvation mode" and conserves energy.

Instead, focus on consuming nutrient dense foods that support a healthy metabolism. This includes incorporating lean proteins, whole grains, fruits, vegetables, and spices into your meals. Foods rich in protein require more energy to digest, which can temporarily increase your metabolic rate. Whole grains provide complex carbohydrates that take longer to break down and can help sustain energy levels.

Spices like cayenne pepper and cinnamon have been shown to have a thermogenic effect, meaning they can temporarily boost metabolic rate. Adding these spices to your dishes can not only enhance flavor but also promote a healthy metabolism.

Additionally, staying properly hydrated is essential for maintaining optimal metabolic function. Drinking enough water helps your body efficiently break down and utilize nutrients from food. Aim to drink at least 8 cups (64 ounces) of water per day or more if you engage in intense physical activity.

By understanding the role of metabolism in weight loss and implementing these dietary strategies, you can support your body's natural calorie burning processes and enhance your overall health. Remember, while metabolism is influenced by various factors, it is within your power to make choices that positively impact your metabolic rate and promote weight loss.

The Science behind the Dash Diet's Effect on Metabolism

Exploring the metabolic benefits of the Dash diet can provide valuable insights into how this eating plan can enhance weight loss and promote overall health. Scientific research has consistently supported the idea that following the Dash diet can have a positive impact on metabolism.

One key aspect of the Dash diet that contributes to its metabolism boosting effects is its emphasis on nutrient dense foods. The diet encourages the consumption of lean proteins, whole grains, fruits, vegetables, and low fat dairy products, all of which contain essential nutrients and compounds necessary for optimal metabolic function.

For example, lean proteins like chicken, fish, and legumes are not only important for muscle growth and repair but also require more energy to digest compared to processed meats high in saturated fats. This thermic effect of food can temporarily increase metabolic rate and contribute to calorie burning.

In addition to lean proteins, whole grains play a vital role in supporting a healthy metabolism. Whole grains, such as quinoa, brown rice, and whole wheat bread, are rich in fiber and complex carbohydrates. These nutrients help regulate blood sugar levels and prevent insulin resistance, which can lead to weight gain and a sluggish metabolism.

Fruits and vegetables are another essential component of the Dash diet that supports metabolic health. These foods are low in calories but high in fiber, vitamins, minerals, and antioxidants. They help maintain a healthy weight by providing satiety without excessive calorie intake. Moreover, certain fruits and vegetables contain compounds like catechins in green tea or capsaicin in chili peppers that can slightly increase metabolism by promoting fat oxidation.

Furthermore, the Dash diet's emphasis on reducing sodium intake can indirectly support a healthy metabolism. High sodium diets can lead to water retention and bloating, making individuals feel sluggish and less energetic. By following the Dash diet's recommendations for low sodium intake, individuals can maintain proper fluid balance, which is essential for a well functioning metabolism.

In summary, scientific research consistently demonstrates the metabolic benefits of following the Dash diet. By emphasizing nutrient dense foods, such as lean proteins, whole grains, fruits, and vegetables, the Dash diet supports optimal metabolic function and helps regulate blood sugar levels. Additionally, reducing sodium intake can indirectly benefit metabolism by promoting healthy fluid balance. By adopting the Dash diet and incorporating its metabolism boosting principles into your daily meals, you can enhance weight loss and support long term health goals.

Incorporating Metabolism Boosting Foods into Your Dash Diet

Now that you understand the importance of metabolism in weight loss, it's time to explore how you can enhance your metabolic rate through specific foods that naturally boost metabolism. By incorporating these metabolism boosting foods into your Dash diet, you can optimize your weight loss efforts and achieve your goals more effectively.

Here is a list of specific foods that naturally enhance metabolism and align with the principles of the Dash diet:

1. Lean Proteins: Foods like skinless chicken breast, turkey, fish, tofu, and legumes are excellent sources of lean protein. They require more energy to digest and metabolize compared to carbohydrates or fats, thereby increasing your metabolic rate.

2. Whole Grains: Choose whole grain options like brown rice, quinoa, oats, and whole wheat bread. These complex carbohydrates provide sustained energy and require more energy to break down, thus supporting a healthy metabolism.

3. Spices: Certain spices have been shown to have thermogenic properties, meaning they can slightly increase your metabolic rate. Incorporate spices like cayenne pepper, ginger, cinnamon, and turmeric into your recipes for an added metabolic boost.

4. Green Tea: Rich in antioxidants and catechins, green tea has been found to stimulate fat oxidation and increase metabolic rate. Enjoy a cup of green tea as part of your daily routine.

5. Hot Peppers: Capsaicin, the compound responsible for the heat in chili peppers, has been shown to temporarily increase metabolism. Add a kick to your meals by incorporating spicy peppers like jalapenos or red chili flakes.

6. High Fiber Foods: Foods rich in fiber, such as fruits, vegetables, and whole grains, require more energy to digest and can help regulate blood sugar levels. This helps maintain a stable metabolism and aids in weight management.

7. Omega3 Fatty Acids: Found in fatty fish like salmon, mackerel, and sardines, as well as flaxseeds and walnuts, omega3 fatty acids support a healthy metabolism and have numerous other health benefits.

Now that you know which foods can naturally enhance your metabolism, it's time to incorporate them into your Dash diet. Here are some recipe and meal ideas featuring these metabolism boosting ingredients:

Grilled chicken with quinoa and roasted vegetables: This balanced meal combines lean protein, whole grains, and fiber rich vegetables for a satisfying and metabolism boosting dinner.

Oatmeal topped with berries and a sprinkle of cinnamon: Starting your day with a bowl of oatmeal provides long lasting energy while the berries add antioxidants and the cinnamon boosts your metabolism.

Vegetable stir fry with tofu: This quick and flavorful stir fry incorporates a variety of vegetables and protein packed tofu for a nutritious and metabolism boosting meal.

By incorporating these metabolism boosting foods into your Dash diet throughout the day, you can maximize the impact on your metabolic rate. Remember to keep portion sizes in mind and maintain a balanced approach to ensure overall health and weight loss success.

Maximizing Physical Activity to Boost Metabolism:

Maintaining a healthy metabolism goes beyond just the foods we eat. Regular physical activity plays a crucial role in optimizing metabolic rate and supporting weight loss. By incorporating various types of exercise into your daily routine, you can enhance the effectiveness of the Dash diet and achieve your weight loss goals more efficiently.

Cardiovascular exercises, such as jogging, cycling, or swimming, are known for their ability to increase heart rate and burn calories. Engaging in cardio workouts not only helps you shed pounds but also boosts your metabolism for hours after the workout. Aim for at least 150 minutes of moderate intensity aerobic activity or 75 minutes of vigorous intensity aerobic activity per week.

Strength training is another essential component of boosting metabolism. Building lean muscle mass through resistance exercises, such as lifting weights or practicing bodyweight exercises like pushups and squats, can elevate your resting metabolic rate. Muscle tissue uses more energy than fat tissue, meaning that the more muscle you have, the more calories you burn even at rest.

Incorporate resistance training into your weekly exercise routine, aiming for sessions two to three times a week. Focus on engaging different muscle groups and gradually increasing the intensity or weight lifted over time. Don't worry about becoming bulky; strength training for women and men offers numerous benefits, including increased bone density and improved body composition.

To make physical activity enjoyable and sustainable, find activities that you genuinely enjoy. Experiment with different exercises and workouts until you discover what feels right for you. Consider joining group fitness classes or finding a workout buddy to help keep you motivated and accountable.

Remember to listen to your body and take rest days when needed. Pushing yourself too hard without adequate recovery can lead to injury or burnout. Choose activities that mix up intensity levels and incorporate both high impact and low impact exercises to prevent overuse injuries.

Lastly, incorporate movement throughout your day whenever possible. Take breaks from sitting for prolonged periods and engage in light activities like stretching or walking. Small bursts of movement can add up and contribute to an overall increase in daily physical activity.

By incorporating a variety of exercises into your routine, you'll not only optimize your metabolism but also experience the numerous benefits of regular physical activity, such as improved cardiovascular health, increased energy levels, and enhanced mood. Remember to consult with a healthcare professional before starting any new exercise program, especially if you have underlying health conditions.

Lifestyle Factors That Support a Healthy Metabolism

Our lifestyle habits have a significant impact on our metabolism, and making positive changes in these areas can help enhance weight loss and overall health. In this section, we will explore the lifestyle factors that influence metabolism and provide strategies for improving them to support a healthy metabolism while following the Dash diet.

One crucial lifestyle habit that affects metabolism is sleep quality. Poor sleep can disrupt metabolic processes, leading to imbalances in hunger hormones and increased cravings for unhealthy foods. To optimize your sleep patterns, try to establish a consistent sleep schedule by going to bed and waking up at the same time each day. Create a relaxing bedtime routine by avoiding stimulating activities before bed and creating a calm environment in your bedroom. Limit exposure to bright screens and electronic devices in the evening, as they can interfere with the natural sleep wake cycle. Additionally, ensure your sleep environment is comfortable, dark, and quiet to promote restful sleep.

Managing stress is another vital aspect of supporting a healthy metabolism. Chronic stress triggers the release of cortisol, a hormone that can lead to increased appetite and cravings for high calorie foods. Find stress management techniques that work for you, such as deep breathing exercises, meditation, yoga, or engaging in hobbies or activities that bring you joy. Incorporate regular relaxation practices into your daily routine to reduce stress levels and support a balanced metabolism.

Staying hydrated is also important for maintaining a healthy metabolism. Dehydration can slow down metabolic processes and make weight loss more challenging. Aim to drink an adequate amount of water throughout the day and listen to your body's thirst cues. Keep a reusable water bottle with you at all times as a reminder to stay hydrated. Infusing water with fresh fruits or herbs can add flavor and encourage you to drink more water throughout the day.

Creating a balanced lifestyle that complements the Dash diet is crucial for long-term success. Focus on finding joy in physical activity by incorporating activities you enjoy into your routine. Whether it's dancing, hiking, swimming, or practicing yoga, finding activities that you love will make it easier to stay active consistently. Remember that small changes can add up over time, so aim for consistency rather than perfection.

Incorporating stress management techniques, improving sleep quality, and staying hydrated are all vital components of supporting a healthy metabolism. By prioritizing these lifestyle factors alongside following the Dash diet, you'll create a well-rounded approach to weight loss and overall health. Remember, achieving a healthy metabolism is not only about what you eat but also how you live your life.

BREAK FAST

A. Overnight Oats

BERRY BANANA OVERNIGHT OATS

Prep: 10 mins | Cook: 3 hours | Serves: 1 loaf

INGREDIENTS

- 100g rolled oats
- 300g Greek yogurt
- 2 ripe bananas, mashed
- 150g mixed berries (e.g., strawberries, blueberries, raspberries)
- 1 tbsp chia seeds
- 1 tbsp flaxseeds
- 250ml milk (or nondairy milk)
- 50g honey
- 1 tsp vanilla extract

INSTRUCTIONS

1. In a large bowl, combine the rolled oats, Greek yogurt, mashed bananas, mixed berries, chia seeds, and flaxseeds.
2. Stir in the milk, honey, and vanilla extract.
3. Pour the mixture into a loaf tin and cover with foil.
4. Refrigerate for at least 3 hours or overnight.
5. In the morning, remove the foil and serve the overnight oats with additional milk or yogurt, if desired.

Tips: You can customize this recipe with different fruits, such as apple cinnamon, pumpkin spice, or strawberry cheesecake.

Nutritional Info: Calories: 250 | Fat: 3g | Carbs: 47g | Protein: 9g

PIÑA COLADA OVERNIGHT OATS

Prep: 10 mins | Cook: 3 hours | Serves: 1 loaf

INGREDIENTS

- 100g rolled oats
- 300g Greek yogurt
- 2 ripe bananas, mashed
- 150g pineapple (canned or fresh), diced
- 1 tbsp chia seeds
- 1 tbsp flaxseeds
- 250ml milk (or nondairy milk)
- 50g honey
- 1 tsp vanilla extract
- 1 tbsp rum (optional)

INSTRUCTIONS

1. In a large bowl, combine the rolled oats, Greek yogurt, mashed bananas, diced pineapple, chia seeds, and flaxseeds.
2. Stir in the milk, honey, vanilla extract, and rum (if using).
3. Pour the mixture into a loaf tin and cover with foil.
4. Refrigerate for at least 3 hours or overnight.
5. In the morning, remove the foil and serve the overnight oats with additional milk or yogurt, if desired.

Tips: For a more authentic piña colada flavor, you can add a splash of coconut milk or coconut water instead of regular milk.

Nutritional Info: Calories: 250 | Fat: 3g | Carbs: 47g | Protein: 9g

CHOCOLATE CHERRY OVERNIGHT OATS

Prep: 10 mins | Cook: 3 hours | Serves: 1 loaf

INGREDIENTS

- 100g rolled oats
- 300g Greek yogurt
- 2 ripe bananas, mashed
- 150g cherries (fresh or frozen), pitted and halved
- 1 tbsp chia seeds
- 1 tbsp flaxseeds
- 250ml milk (or nondairy milk)
- 50g honey
- 1 tsp vanilla extract
- 2 tbsp cocoa powder

INSTRUCTIONS

1. In a large bowl, combine the rolled oats, Greek yogurt, mashed bananas, cherries, chia seeds, and flaxseeds.
2. Stir in the milk, honey, vanilla extract, and cocoa powder.
3. Pour the mixture into a loaf tin and cover with foil.
4. Refrigerate for at least 3 hours or overnight.
5. In the morning, remove the foil and serve the overnight oats with additional milk or yogurt, if desired.

Tips: You can also add a handful of chocolate chips or cocoa nibs for extra chocolate flavor.

Nutritional Info: Calories: 250 | Fat: 3g | Carbs: 47g | Protein: 9g

CARROT CAKE OVERNIGHT OATS

Prep: 10 mins | Cook: 3 hours | Serves: 1 loaf

INGREDIENTS

- 100g rolled oats
- 300g Greek yogurt
- 2 ripe bananas, mashed
- 150g carrots (grated)
- 1 tbsp chia seeds
- 1 tbsp flaxseeds
- 250ml milk (or nondairy milk)
- 50g honey
- 1 tsp vanilla extract
- 1 tsp ground cinnamon

INSTRUCTIONS

1. In a large bowl, combine the rolled oats, Greek yogurt, mashed bananas, grated carrots, chia seeds, and flaxseeds.
2. Stir in the milk, honey, vanilla extract, and ground cinnamon.
3. Pour the mixture into a loaf tin and cover with foil.
4. Refrigerate for at least 3 hours or overnight.
5. In the morning, remove the foil and serve the overnight oats with additional milk or yogurt, if desired.

Tips: You can add a handful of chopped walnuts or pecans for extra crunch.

Nutritional Info: Calories: 250 | Fat: 3g | Carbs: 47g | Protein: 9g

APPLE CINNAMON OVERNIGHT OATS

Prep: 10 mins | Cook: 3 hours | Serves: 1 loaf

INGREDIENTS

- 100g rolled oats
- 300g Greek yogurt
- 2 ripe bananas, mashed
- 1 apple (cored and sliced)
- 1 tbsp chia seeds
- 1 tbsp flaxseeds
- 250ml milk (or nondairy milk)
- 50g honey
- 1 tsp vanilla extract
- 1 tsp ground cinnamon

INSTRUCTIONS

1. In a large bowl, combine the rolled oats, Greek yogurt, mashed bananas, sliced apple, chia seeds, and flaxseeds.
2. Stir in the milk, honey, vanilla extract, and ground cinnamon.
3. Pour the mixture into a loaf tin and cover with foil.
4. Refrigerate for at least 3 hours or overnight.
5. In the morning, remove the foil and serve the overnight oats

with additional milk or yogurt, if desired.

Tips: You can use any type of apple you like, but Granny Smith apples add a nice tartness to the oats.

Nutritional Info: Calories: 250 | Fat: 3g | Carbs: 47g | Protein: 9g

PUMPKIN SPICE OVERNIGHT OATS

Prep: 10 mins | Cook: 3 hours | Serves: 1 loaf

INGREDIENTS

- 100g rolled oats
- 300g Greek yogurt
- 2 ripe bananas, mashed
- 150g pumpkin puree
- 1 tbsp chia seeds
- 1 tbsp flaxseeds
- 250ml milk (or nondairy milk)
- 50g honey
- 1 tsp vanilla extract
- 1 tsp pumpkin pie spice

INSTRUCTIONS

1. In a large bowl, combine the rolled oats, Greek yogurt, mashed bananas, pumpkin puree, chia seeds, and flaxseeds.
2. Stir in the milk, honey, vanilla extract, and pumpkin pie spice.
3. Pour the mixture into a loaf tin and cover with foil.

4. Refrigerate for at least 3 hours or overnight.
5. In the morning, remove the foil and serve the overnight oats with additional milk or yogurt, if desired.

Tips: You can top the oats with chopped nuts or a drizzle of maple syrup for extra flavor.

Nutritional Info: Calories: 250 | Fat: 3g | Carbs: 47g | Protein: 9g

STRAWBERRY CHEESECAKE OVERNIGHT OATS

Prep: 10 mins | Cook: 3 hours | Serves: 1 loaf

INGREDIENTS

- 100g rolled oats
- 300g Greek yogurt
- 2 ripe bananas, mashed
- 150g strawberries, diced
- 1 tbsp chia seeds
- 1 tbsp flaxseeds
- 250ml milk (or nondairy milk)
- 50g honey
- 1 tsp vanilla extract
- 50g cream cheese, softened

INSTRUCTIONS

1. In a large bowl, combine the rolled oats, Greek yogurt, mashed bananas, diced strawberries, chia seeds, and flaxseeds.
2. Stir in the milk, honey, vanilla extract, and softened cream cheese.
3. Pour the mixture into a loaf tin and cover with foil.
4. Refrigerate for at least 3 hours or overnight.
5. In the morning, remove the foil and serve the overnight oats with additional diced strawberries, if desired.

Tips: You can use any type of berry you like, such as blueberries or raspberries.

Nutritional Info: Calories: 250 | Fat: 3g | Carbs: 47g | Protein: 9g

BLUEBERRY MUFFIN OVERNIGHT OATS

Prep: 10 mins | Cook: 3 hours | Serves: 1 loaf

INGREDIENTS

- 100g rolled oats
- 300g Greek yogurt
- 2 ripe bananas, mashed
- 150g blueberries
- 1 tbsp chia seeds
- 1 tbsp flaxseeds
- 250ml milk (or nondairy milk)
- 50g honey
- 1 tsp vanilla extract
- 1 tsp ground cinnamon

INSTRUCTIONS

1. In a large bowl, combine the rolled oats, Greek yogurt, mashed bananas, blueberries, chia seeds, and flaxseeds.
2. Stir in the milk, honey, vanilla extract, and ground cinnamon.
3. Pour the mixture into a loaf tin and cover with foil.
4. Refrigerate for at least 3 hours or overnight.
5. In the morning, remove the foil and serve the overnight oats with additional blueberries, if desired.

Tips: You can add a handful of chopped nuts or a drizzle of honey for extra sweetness.

Nutritional Info: Calories: 250 | Fat: 3g | Carbs: 47g | Protein: 9g

Tips: You can use almond butter or another nut butter instead of peanut butter.

Nutritional Info: Calories: 250 | Fat: 3g | Carbs: 47g | Protein: 9g

CHOCOLATE PEANUT BUTTER

OVERNIGHT OATS

Prep: 10 mins | Cook: 3 hours | Serves: 1 loaf

INGREDIENTS

- 100g rolled oats
- 300g Greek yogurt
- 2 ripe bananas, mashed
- 2 tbsp peanut butter
- 1 tbsp chia seeds
- 1 tbsp flaxseeds
- 250ml milk (or nondairy milk)
- 50g honey
- 1 tsp vanilla extract
- 2 tbsp cocoa powder

INSTRUCTIONS

1. In a large bowl, combine the rolled oats, Greek yogurt, mashed bananas, peanut butter, chia seeds, and flaxseeds.
2. Stir in the milk, honey, vanilla extract, and cocoa powder.
3. Pour the mixture into a loaf tin and cover with foil.
4. Refrigerate for at least 3 hours or overnight.
5. In the morning, remove the foil and serve the overnight oats with additional peanut butter or chocolate chips, if desired.

LEMON POPPYSEED OVERNIGHT OATS

Prep: 10 mins | Cook: 3 hours | Serves: 1 loaf

INGREDIENTS

- 100g rolled oats
- 300g Greek yogurt
- 2 ripe bananas, mashed
- 1 lemon (zested and juiced)
- 1 tbsp chia seeds
- 1 tbsp flaxseeds
- 250ml milk (or nondairy milk)
- 50g honey
- 1 tsp vanilla extract
- 1 tbsp poppyseeds

INSTRUCTIONS

1. In a large bowl, combine the rolled oats, Greek yogurt, mashed bananas, lemon zest and juice, chia seeds, and flaxseeds.
2. Stir in the milk, honey, vanilla extract, and poppyseeds.
3. Pour the mixture into a loaf tin and cover with foil.
4. Refrigerate for at least 3 hours or overnight.
5. In the morning, remove the foil and serve the overnight oats with additional lemon zest or poppyseeds, if desired.

Tips: You can add a drizzle of honey or maple syrup for extra sweetness.

Nutritional Info: Calories: 250 | Fat: 3g | Carbs: 47g | Protein: 9g

B. Egg dishes

HAM AND CHEESE EGG CUPS

Prep: 10 mins | Cook: 20 mins | Serves: 6

INGREDIENTS

- 6 large eggs
- 50g ham, diced
- 50g cheddar cheese, grated
- 50g spinach, chopped
- Salt and pepper, to taste

INSTRUCTIONS

1. Preheat the oven to 180°C (350°F) and grease a muffin tin.
2. In a large bowl, whisk the eggs and season with salt and pepper.
3. Stir in the diced ham, grated cheese, and chopped spinach.
4. Pour the mixture into the muffin tin, filling each cup about 3/4 full.
5. Bake for 20 minutes or until the egg cups are set and golden brown.
6. Remove from the oven and let cool for a few minutes before serving.

Tips: You can use any type of cheese or meat you like, such as feta cheese or cooked bacon.

Nutritional Info: Calories: 150 | Fat: 10g | Carbs: 1g | Protein: 13g

SAUSAGE AND CHEESE EGG CUPS

Prep: 10 mins | Cook: 20 mins | Serves: 6

INGREDIENTS

- 6 large eggs
- 50g sausage, cooked and crumbled
- 50g cheddar cheese, grated
- 50g bell pepper, diced
- Salt and pepper, to taste

INSTRUCTIONS

1. Preheat the oven to 180°C (350°F) and grease a muffin tin.
2. In a large bowl, whisk the eggs and season with salt and pepper.
3. Stir in the cooked and crumbled sausage, grated cheese, and diced bell pepper.
4. Pour the mixture into the muffin tin, filling each cup about 3/4 full.
5. Bake for 20 minutes or until the egg cups are set and golden brown.
6. Remove from the oven and let cool for a few minutes before serving.

Tips: You can use any type of sausage or cheese you like, such as turkey sausage or mozzarella cheese.

Nutritional Info: Calories: 150 | Fat: 10g | Carbs: 1g | Protein: 13g

SPINACH AND TOMATO EGG CUPS

Prep: 10 mins | Cook: 20 mins | Serves: 6

INGREDIENTS

- 6 large eggs
- 50g cherry tomatoes, halved
- 50g spinach, chopped
- 50g feta cheese, crumbled
- Salt and pepper, to taste

INSTRUCTIONS

1. Preheat the oven to 180°C (350°F) and grease a muffin tin.
2. In a large bowl, whisk the eggs and season with salt and pepper.
3. Stir in the halved cherry tomatoes, chopped spinach, and crumbled feta cheese.
4. Pour the mixture into the muffin tin, filling each cup about 3/4 full.
5. Bake for 20 minutes or until the egg cups are set and golden brown.
6. Remove from the oven and let cool for a few minutes before serving.

Tips: You can use any type of cheese you like, such as goat cheese or cheddar cheese.

Nutritional Info: Calories: 150 | Fat: 10g | Carbs: 1g | Protein: 13g

BROCCOLI AND CHEDDAR EGG CUPS

Prep: 10 mins | Cook: 20 mins | Serves: 6

INGREDIENTS

- 6 large eggs
- 50g broccoli, chopped
- 50g cheddar cheese, grated
- 50g onion, diced
- Salt and pepper, to taste

INSTRUCTIONS

1. Preheat the oven to 180°C (350°F) and grease a muffin tin.
2. In a large bowl, whisk the eggs and season with salt and pepper.
3. Stir in the chopped broccoli, grated cheese, and diced onion.
4. Pour the mixture into the muffin tin, filling each cup about 3/4 full.
5. Bake for 20 minutes or until the egg cups are set and golden brown.
6. Remove from the oven and let cool for a few minutes before serving.

Tips: You can use any type of vegetable or cheese you like, such as zucchini or feta cheese.

Nutritional Info: Calories: 150 | Fat: 10g | Carbs: 1g | Protein: 13g

BELL PEPPER EGG CUPS

Prep: 10 mins | Cook: 20 mins | Serves: 6

INGREDIENTS

- 6 large eggs
- 50g bell pepper, diced
- 50g onion, diced
- 50g cheddar cheese, grated
- Salt and pepper, to taste

INSTRUCTIONS

1. Preheat the oven to 180°C (350°F) and grease a muffin tin.
2. In a large bowl, whisk the eggs and season with salt and pepper.
3. Stir in the diced bell pepper, diced onion, and grated cheese.
4. Pour the mixture into the muffin tin, filling each cup about 3/4 full.
5. Bake for 20 minutes or until the egg cups are set and golden brown.
6. Remove from the oven and let cool for a few minutes before serving.

Tips: You can use any type of cheese you like, such as mozzarella or feta cheese.

Nutritional Info: Calories: 150 | Fat: 10g | Carbs: 1g | Protein: 13g

MUSHROOM AND ONION EGG CUPS

Prep: 10 mins | Cook: 20 mins | Serves: 6

INGREDIENTS

- 6 large eggs
- 50g mushrooms, chopped
- 50g onion, diced
- 50g cheddar cheese, grated
- Salt and pepper, to taste

INSTRUCTIONS

1. Preheat the oven to 180°C (350°F) and grease a muffin tin.
2. In a large bowl, whisk the eggs and season with salt and pepper.
3. Stir in the chopped mushrooms and diced onion.
4. Pour the mixture into the muffin tin, filling each cup about 3/4 full.
5. Bake for 20 minutes or until the egg cups are set and golden brown.
6. Remove from the oven and let cool for a few minutes before serving.

Tips: You can use any type of cheese you like, such as mozzarella or feta cheese.

Nutritional Info: Calories: 150 | Fat: 10g | Carbs: 1g | Protein: 13g

BACON AND SCALLION EGG CUPS

Prep: 10 mins | Cook: 20 mins | Serves: 6

INGREDIENTS

- 6 large eggs
- 50g bacon, cooked and crumbled
- 50g scallions, chopped
- 50g cheddar cheese, grated
- Salt and pepper, to taste

INSTRUCTIONS

1. Preheat the oven to 180°C (350°F) and grease a muffin tin.
2. In a large bowl, whisk the eggs and season with salt and pepper.
3. Stir in the cooked and crumbled bacon, chopped scallions, and grated cheese.
4. Pour the mixture into the muffin tin, filling each cup about 3/4 full.
5. Bake for 20 minutes or until the egg cups are set and golden brown.
6. Remove from the oven and let cool for a few minutes before serving.

Tips: You can use any type of cheese you like, such as goat cheese or feta cheese.

Nutritional Info: Calories: 150 | Fat: 10g | Carbs: 1g | Protein: 13g

EGG WHITE FRITTATAS

Prep: 10 mins | Cook: 20 mins | Serves: 6

INGREDIENTS

- 6 large eggs, separated
- 50g spinach, chopped
- 50g cherry tomatoes, halved
- 50g cheddar cheese, grated
- Salt and pepper, to taste

INSTRUCTIONS

1. Preheat the oven to 180°C (350°F) and grease a muffin tin.
2. In a large bowl, whisk the egg whites until frothy.
3. Stir in the chopped spinach, halved tomatoes, and grated cheese.
4. Pour the mixture into the muffin tin, filling each cup about 3/4 full.
5. Bake for 20 minutes or until the frittatas are set and golden brown.
6. Remove from the oven and let cool for a few minutes before serving.

Tips: You can use any type of cheese you like, such as mozzarella or feta cheese.

Nutritional Info: Calories: 150 | Fat: 10g | Carbs: 1g | Protein: 13g

ZUCCHINI EGG FRITTATAS

Prep: 10 mins | Cook: 20 mins | Serves: 6

INGREDIENTS

- 6 large eggs, separated
- 50g zucchini, grated
- 50g cherry tomatoes, halved
- 50g cheddar cheese, grated
- Salt and pepper, to taste

INSTRUCTIONS

1. Preheat the oven to 180°C (350°F) and grease a muffin tin.
2. In a large bowl, whisk the egg whites until frothy.
3. Stir in the grated zucchini, halved tomatoes, and grated cheese.
4. Pour the mixture into the muffin tin, filling each cup about 3/4 full.
5. Bake for 20 minutes or until the frittatas are set and golden brown.
6. Remove from the oven and let cool for a few minutes before serving.

Tips: You can use any type of cheese you like, such as mozzarella or feta cheese.

Nutritional Info: Calories: 150 | Fat: 10g | Carbs: 1g | Protein: 13g

ROASTED VEGETABLE EGG FRITTATAS

Prep: 10 mins | Cook: 20 mins | Serves: 6

INGREDIENTS

- 6 large eggs, separated
- 50g mixed vegetables (e.g., bell peppers, onions, tomatoes), chopped
- 50g cheddar cheese, grated
- Salt and pepper, to taste

INSTRUCTIONS

1. Preheat the oven to 180°C (350°F) and grease a muffin tin.
2. In a large bowl, whisk the egg whites until frothy.
3. Stir in the chopped mixed vegetables and grated cheese.
4. Pour the mixture into the muffin tin, filling each cup about 3/4 full.
5. Bake for 20 minutes or until the frittatas are set and golden brown.
6. Remove from the oven and let cool for a few minutes before serving.

Tips: You can use any type of cheese you like, such as mozzarella or feta cheese.

Nutritional Info: Calories: 150 | Fat: 10g | Carbs: 1g | Protein: 13g

LUNCH

Salad

CHICKEN CAESAR SALAD

Prep: 15 mins | Cook: 15 mins | Serves: 4

INGREDIENTS

- 400g boneless, skinless chicken breasts
- 1 head of romaine lettuce, chopped
- 50g croutons
- 50g parmesan cheese, grated
- 1/4 cup olive oil
- 2 tbsp lemon juice
- 1 tbsp dijon mustard
- 1 garlic clove, minced
- Salt and pepper, to taste

INSTRUCTIONS

1. Preheat the oven to 200°C (400°F) and line a baking sheet with parchment paper.
2. Season the chicken breasts with salt and pepper and place them on the baking sheet.
3. Bake for 15 minutes or until the chicken is cooked through.
4. In a large bowl, whisk together the olive oil, lemon juice, dijon mustard, minced garlic, salt, and pepper.
5. Add the chopped romaine lettuce to the bowl and toss to coat with the dressing.
6. Divide the lettuce among four plates and top with sliced chicken, croutons, and grated parmesan cheese.

Tips: You can use any type of lettuce you like, such as kale or spinach.

Nutritional Info: Calories: 350 | Fat: 20g | Carbs: 10g | Protein: 30g

COBB SALAD

Prep: 15 mins | Cook: 15 mins | Serves: 4

INGREDIENTS

- 400g boneless, skinless chicken breasts
- 4 slices of bacon, cooked and crumbled
- 2 hardboiled eggs, chopped
- 1 avocado, diced
- 1 head of romaine lettuce, chopped
- 50g cherry tomatoes, halved
- 50g blue cheese, crumbled
- 1/4 cup olive oil
- 2 tbsp red wine vinegar
- 1 tsp dijon mustard
- Salt and pepper, to taste

Tips: You can use any type of cheese you like, such as feta or cheddar cheese.

Nutritional Info: Calories: 400 | Fat: 25g | Carbs: 10g | Protein: 35g

INSTRUCTIONS

1. Preheat the oven to 200°C (400°F) and line a baking sheet with parchment paper.
2. Season the chicken breasts with salt and pepper and place them on the baking sheet.
3. Bake for 15 minutes or until the chicken is cooked through.
4. In a large bowl, whisk together the olive oil, red wine vinegar, dijon mustard, salt, and pepper.
5. Add the chopped romaine lettuce to the bowl and toss to coat with the dressing.
6. Divide the lettuce among four plates and top with sliced chicken, crumbled bacon, chopped hardboiled eggs, diced avocado, halved cherry tomatoes, and crumbled blue cheese.

GREEK SALAD

Prep: 15 mins | Cook: 0 mins | Serves: 4

INGREDIENTS

- 1 head of romaine lettuce, chopped
- 50g cherry tomatoes, halved
- 50g cucumber, diced
- 50g red onion, sliced
- 50g kalamata olives, pitted
- 50g feta cheese, crumbled
- 1/4 cup olive oil
- 2 tbsp red wine vinegar
- 1 tsp dried oregano
- Salt and pepper, to taste

INSTRUCTIONS

1. In a large bowl, whisk together the olive oil, red wine vinegar, dried oregano, salt, and pepper.
2. Add the chopped romaine lettuce, halved cherry tomatoes, diced cucumber, sliced red onion, pitted kalamata olives, and crumbled feta cheese to the bowl and toss to coat with the dressing.
3. Divide the salad among four plates and serve.

Tips: You can add grilled chicken or shrimp for extra protein.

Nutritional Info: Calories: 200 | Fat: 15g | Carbs: 10g | Protein: 5g

STRAWBERRY SPINACH SALAD

Prep: 15 mins | Cook: 0 mins | Serves: 4

INGREDIENTS

- 1 bag of baby spinach
- 200g strawberries, sliced
- 50g red onion, sliced
- 50g feta cheese, crumbled
- 1/4 cup olive oil
- 2 tbsp balsamic vinegar
- 1 tsp dijon mustard
- Salt and pepper, to taste

INSTRUCTIONS

1. In a large bowl, whisk together the olive oil, balsamic vinegar, dijon mustard, salt, and pepper.
2. Add the baby spinach, sliced strawberries, sliced red onion, and crumbled feta cheese to the bowl and toss to coat with the dressing.
3. Divide the salad among four plates and serve.

Tips: You can add grilled chicken or shrimp for extra protein.

Nutritional Info: Calories: 150 | Fat: 10g | Carbs: 10g | Protein: 5g

SOUTHWESTERN QUINOA SALAD

Prep: 15 mins | Cook: 20 mins | Serves: 4

INGREDIENTS

- 200g quinoa
- 400g black beans, drained and rinsed
- 50g corn kernels
- 50g cherry tomatoes, halved
- 50g red onion, diced
- 1 avocado, diced
- 1/4 cup olive oil
- 2 tbsp lime juice
- 1 tsp cumin
- Salt and pepper, to taste

INSTRUCTIONS

1. Cook the quinoa according to package **INSTRUCTIONS** and let cool.
2. In a large bowl, whisk together the olive oil, lime juice, cumin, salt, and pepper.
3. Add the cooked quinoa, drained and rinsed black beans, corn kernels, halved cherry tomatoes, diced red onion, and diced avocado to the bowl and toss to coat with the dressing.
4. Divide the salad among four plates and serve.

Tips: You can add grilled chicken or shrimp for extra protein.

Nutritional Info: Calories: 350 | Fat: 20g | Carbs: 30g | Protein: 10g

AVOCADO AND CHICKPEA SALAD

Prep: 15 mins | Cook: 0 mins | Serves: 4

INGREDIENTS

- 2 avocados, diced
- 400g canned chickpeas, drained and rinsed
- 50g cherry tomatoes, halved
- 50g cucumber, diced
- 50g red onion, sliced
- 1/4 cup olive oil
- 2 tbsp lemon juice
- 1 tsp dijon mustard
- Salt and pepper, to taste

INSTRUCTIONS

1. In a large bowl, whisk together the olive oil, lemon juice, dijon mustard, salt, and pepper.
2. Add the diced avocados, chickpeas, halved cherry tomatoes, diced cucumber, and sliced red onion to the bowl and toss to coat with the dressing.
3. Divide the salad among four plates and serve.

Tips: You can add grilled chicken or shrimp for extra protein.

Nutritional Info: Calories: 250 | Fat: 15g | Carbs: 10g | Protein: 9g

CURRIED CHICKEN SALAD

Prep: 15 mins | Cook: 0 mins | Serves: 4

INGREDIENTS

- 200g boneless, skinless chicken breasts
- 1 tsp curry powder
- 1/4 cup Greek yogurt
- 50g raisins
- 50g chopped apple
- 50g chopped celery
- 50g chopped cashews
- Salt and pepper, to taste

INSTRUCTIONS

1. In a small bowl, mix the curry powder with 1 tbsp of water to create a paste.
2. In a large bowl, combine the Greek yogurt and curry paste to make the dressing.
3. Season the chicken breasts with salt and pepper, and cook in a skillet over medium heat until fully cooked. Let the chicken cool, then shred it.
4. Add the shredded chicken, raisins, chopped apple, chopped celery, and chopped cashews to the bowl with the dressing.
5. Toss to combine and serve.

Tips: You can substitute the Greek yogurt with lowfat mayonnaise if you prefer.

Nutritional Info: Calories: 200 | Fat: 10g | Carbs: 10g | Protein: 30g

TUNA SALAD

Prep: 15 mins | Cook: 0 mins | Serves: 4

INGREDIENTS

- 2 (125g) cans tuna, drained and flaked
- 50g chopped bell peppers
- 50g chopped tomatoes
- 50g chopped cucumber
- 1/4 cup olive oil
- 2 tbsp lemon juice
- 1 tsp dijon mustard
- Salt and pepper, to taste

INSTRUCTIONS

1. In a large bowl, whisk together the olive oil, lemon juice, dijon mustard, salt, and pepper.
2. Add the flaked tuna, chopped bell peppers, chopped tomatoes, and chopped cucumber to the bowl and toss to coat with the dressing.
3. Divide the tuna salad among four plates and serve.

Tips: You can add chopped hardboiled egg or black olives for extra flavor.

Nutritional Info: Calories: 250 | Fat: 15g | Carbs: 4g | Protein: 35g

CHICKEN FAJITA SALAD

Prep: 15 mins | Cook: 0 mins | Serves: 4

INGREDIENTS

- 2 (125g) cans chicken breast, drained and flaked
- 50g chopped bell peppers
- 50g chopped onions
- 50g chopped tomatoes
- 1/4 cup olive oil
- 2 tbsp lemon juice
- 1 tsp dijon mustard
- Salt and pepper, to taste
- 1/2 cup chopped cilantro
- 1/2 cup chopped green onions

INSTRUCTIONS

1. In a large bowl, whisk together the olive oil, lemon juice, dijon mustard, salt, and pepper.
2. Add the flaked chicken, chopped bell peppers, chopped onions, and chopped tomatoes to the bowl and toss to coat with the dressing.
3. Divide the chicken fajita salad among four plates and top with chopped cilantro and green onions.

Tips: You can add chopped avocado or black beans for extra flavor.

Nutritional Info: Calories: 200 | Fat: 10g | Carbs: 4g | Protein: 35g

CAPRESE SALAD

Prep: 15 mins | Cook: 0 mins | Serves: 4

INGREDIENTS

- 100g fresh mozzarella cheese, sliced
- 2 large fresh tomatoes, sliced
- 1/4 cup basil leaves, torn
- 1/4 cup fresh mint leaves, torn
- 1/4 cup olive oil
- Salt and pepper, to taste

INSTRUCTIONS

1. On four plates, arrange the sliced mozzarella cheese, tomato slices, and torn basil and mint leaves.
2. Drizzle with olive oil and season with salt and pepper to taste.

Tips: You can add a balsamic glaze or a simple vinaigrette for extra flavor.

Nutritional Info: Calories: 150 | Fat: 10g | Carbs: 4g | Protein: 10g

Soup

MINESTRONE SOUP

Prep: 15 mins | Cook: 2 hours | Serves: 4

INGREDIENTS

- 1 tbsp (15g) olive oil
- 1 onion, diced
- 2 carrots, diced
- 2 celery stalks, diced
- 2 garlic cloves, minced
- 400g canned kidney beans, drained and rinsed
- 400g canned diced tomatoes
- 1.5L (6 cups) lowsodium vegetable broth
- 100g (1 cup) small pasta
- 50g (1 cup) spinach, chopped
- Salt and pepper, to taste

INSTRUCTIONS

1. Heat olive oil in a large pot over medium heat.
2. Add the diced onion, carrots, and celery. Cook for 57 minutes until the vegetables are softened.
3. Add the minced garlic and cook for an additional 12 minutes.
4. Pour in the vegetable broth, diced tomatoes, and kidney beans. Bring to a boil.
5. Once boiling, add the pasta and cook according to the package instructions.
6. Stir in the chopped spinach and cook until wilted.
7. Season with salt and pepper to taste.

Tips

You can customize the vegetables and beans based on your preference.

This soup can be stored in the fridge for up to 3 days or frozen for up to 3 months.

Nutritional Info

Calories: 250 | Fat: 3g | Carbs: 47g | Protein: 9g

VEGETARIAN CHILI

Prep: 15 mins | Cook: 1.5 hours | Serves: 4

INGREDIENTS

- 1 tbsp (15g) olive oil
- 1 onion, diced
- 2 bell peppers, diced
- 2 garlic cloves, minced
- 400g canned kidney beans, drained and rinsed
- 400g canned black beans, drained and rinsed
- 800g canned diced tomatoes
- 1 tbsp (8g) chili powder
- 1 tsp (2g) cumin
- Salt and pepper, to taste

INSTRUCTIONS

1. Heat olive oil in a large pot over medium heat.
2. Add the diced onion and bell peppers. Cook for 57 minutes until the vegetables are softened.
3. Add the minced garlic, chili powder, and cumin. Cook for an additional 12 minutes.
4. Pour in the diced tomatoes, kidney beans, and black beans. Bring to a boil.
5. Once boiling, reduce the heat and let the chili simmer for 11.5 hours.
6. Season with salt and pepper to taste.

Tips: You can add more vegetables such as corn or zucchini for extra texture.

This chili is great for meal prep and can be stored in the fridge for up to 5 days or frozen for up to 3 months.

Nutritional Info

Calories: 220 | Fat: 2g | Carbs: 40g | Protein: 10g

CHICKEN NOODLE SOUP

Prep: 10 mins | Cook: 30 mins | Serves: 4

INGREDIENTS

- 1 tbsp (15g) olive oil
- 1 onion, diced
- 2 carrots, diced
- 2 celery stalks, diced
- 2 garlic cloves, minced
- 1.5L (6 cups) lowsodium chicken broth
- 200g (2 cups) cooked chicken breast, shredded
- 100g (1 cup) egg noodles
- Salt and pepper, to taste

INSTRUCTIONS

1. Heat olive oil in a large pot over medium heat.
2. Add the diced onion, carrots, and celery. Cook for 57 minutes until the vegetables are softened.
3. Add the minced garlic and cook for an additional 12 minutes.
4. Pour in the chicken broth and bring to a boil.
5. Once boiling, add the egg noodles and cook according to the package instructions.
6. Add the shredded chicken to the pot and cook until heated through.
7. Season with salt and pepper to taste.

Tips: You can add more vegetables such as peas or corn for extra texture.

This soup can be stored in the fridge for up to 3 days or frozen for up to 3 months.

Nutritional Info: Calories: 250 | Fat: 3g | Carbs: 20g | Protein: 30g

VEGETABLE LENTIL SOUP

Prep: 10 mins | Cook: 45 mins | Serves: 4

INGREDIENTS

- 1 tbsp (15g) olive oil
- 1 onion, diced
- 2 carrots, diced
- 2 celery stalks, diced
- 2 garlic cloves, minced
- 1L (4 cups) lowsodium vegetable broth
- 200g (1 cup) dried lentils, rinsed and drained
- 400g canned diced tomatoes
- 1 tsp (2g) cumin
- Salt and pepper, to taste

INSTRUCTIONS

1. Heat olive oil in a large pot over medium heat.
2. Add the diced onion, carrots, and celery. Cook for 57 minutes until the vegetables are softened.
3. Add the minced garlic and cook for an additional 12 minutes.
4. Pour in the vegetable broth and bring to a boil.
5. Once boiling, add the lentils, canned diced tomatoes, and cumin. Reduce the heat and let the soup simmer for 3040 minutes until the lentils are tender.
6. Season with salt and pepper to taste.

Tips

You can add more vegetables such as zucchini or spinach for extra nutrition.

This soup can be stored in the fridge for up to 3 days or frozen for up to 3 months.

Nutritional Info

Calories: 200

Fat: 3g

Carbs: 30g

Protein: 15g

BEEF AND BARLEY SOUP

Prep: 15 mins | Cook: 1.5 hours | Serves: 4

INGREDIENTS

- 200g (1 cup) beef stew meat, cubed
- 100g (1/2 cup) pearl barley
- 1 onion, diced
- 2 carrots, diced
- 2 celery stalks, diced
- 2 garlic cloves, minced
- 1.5L (6 cups) lowsodium beef broth
- 2 bay leaves
- Salt and pepper, to taste

INSTRUCTIONS

1. In a large pot, brown the beef stew meat over mediumhigh heat.
2. Add the diced onion, carrots, and celery. Cook for 57 minutes until the vegetables are softened.
3. Add the minced garlic and cook for an additional 12 minutes.
4. Pour in the beef broth and add the pearl barley and bay leaves. Bring to a boil.
5. Once boiling, reduce the heat and let the soup simmer for 11.5 hours until the beef is tender and the barley is cooked.
6. Season with salt and pepper to taste.

Tips: For a thicker soup, add more barley.

This soup can be stored in the fridge for up to 3 days or frozen for up to 3 months.

Nutritional Info

Calories: 250

Fat: 3g

Carbs: 30g

Protein: 20g

BROCCOLI CHEDDAR SOUP

Prep: 10 mins | Cook: 30 mins | Serves: 4

INGREDIENTS

- 450g broccoli, chopped (4 cups)
- 1 medium onion, chopped
- 2 garlic cloves, minced
- 4 cups (946g) lowsodium chicken or vegetable broth
- 1 cup (240ml) skim milk
- 1/4 cup (30g) allpurpose flour
- 1 1/2 cups (170g) shredded cheddar cheese
- 2 tbsp (30g) unsalted butter
- Salt and pepper to taste

INSTRUCTIONS

1. In a large pot, melt the butter over medium heat.
2. Add the chopped onion and garlic, and sauté for 34 minutes until softened.
3. Sprinkle the flour over the onion and garlic, and cook for 12 minutes, stirring constantly.
4. Gradually whisk in the chicken or vegetable broth, ensuring the flour is well incorporated to avoid lumps.
5. Add the chopped broccoli, and bring the mixture to a boil. Reduce the heat and let it simmer for 1520 minutes, or until the broccoli is tender.
6. Stir in the milk and shredded cheddar cheese, and continue to cook for an additional 510 minutes until the cheese is melted and the soup is heated through.
7. Season with salt and pepper to taste.

Tips

For a smoother soup, you can use an immersion blender to purée the soup before adding the cheese.

Garnish with additional shredded cheddar cheese and a few broccoli florets for a decorative touch.

Nutritional Info

Calories: 250

Fat: 12g | Carbs: 20g | Protein: 15g

TOMATO BASIL SOUP

Prep: 10 mins | Cook: 30 mins | Serves: 4

INGREDIENTS

- 1 tbsp (15ml) olive oil
- 1 onion, chopped
- 2 garlic cloves, minced
- 800g (28oz) canned diced tomatoes
- 2 cups (473ml) lowsodium vegetable broth
- 1/2 cup (120ml) skim milk
- 1/4 cup (10g) fresh basil leaves, chopped
- Salt and pepper to taste

INSTRUCTIONS

1. In a large pot, heat the olive oil over medium heat.
2. Add the chopped onion and garlic, and sauté for 34 minutes until softened.
3. Add the canned diced tomatoes and vegetable broth, and bring the mixture to a boil.
4. Reduce the heat and let the soup simmer for 1520 minutes.
5. Remove the pot from the heat and let it cool slightly.
6. Using an immersion blender, purée the soup until smooth.
7. Stir in the skim milk and chopped basil leaves, and heat the soup over low heat until heated through.
8. Season with salt and pepper to taste.

Tips

For a creamier soup, you can add more skim milk or even a dollop of Greek yogurt.

Garnish with additional chopped basil leaves and a drizzle of olive oil for a pop of color and flavor.

Nutritional Info

Calories: 120

Fat: 3g

Carbs: 20g

Protein: 5g

CHICKEN TORTILLA SOUP

Prep: 15 mins | Cook: 25 mins | Serves: 8

INGREDIENTS

- 1 tbsp (15ml) olive oil
- 1 onion, chopped
- 2 garlic cloves, minced
- 800g (28oz) canned diced tomatoes
- 2 cups (473ml) lowsodium vegetable broth
- 1/2 cup (120ml) skim milk
- 1/4 cup (10g) fresh basil leaves, chopped
- Salt and pepper to taste

INSTRUCTIONS

1. Heat the olive oil in a large pot over medium heat.
2. Sauté the onion and garlic for 34 minutes until softened.
3. Add the canned diced tomatoes and vegetable broth, and bring to a boil.
4. Reduce the heat and let the soup simmer for 1520 minutes.
5. Remove the pot from the heat and let it cool slightly.
6. Use an immersion blender to purée the soup until smooth.
7. Stir in the skim milk and chopped basil leaves, and heat the soup over low heat until heated through.
8. Season with salt and pepper to taste.

Tips : For a creamier soup, you can add more skim milk or a dollop of Greek yogurt.

Garnish with additional chopped basil leaves and a drizzle of olive oil.

Nutritional Info

Calories: 120 | Fat: 3g | Carbs: 20g | Protein: 5g

LOADED BAKED POTATO SOUP

Prep: 15 mins | Cook: 25 mins | Serves: 6

INGREDIENTS

- 4 potatoes, scrubbed
- 8 bacon slices
- 4 tbsp unsalted butter
- 2 garlic cloves, minced
- 1/4 cup yellow onion
- 1/3 cup allpurpose flour
- 2 cups low fat milk
- 1 cup half and half
- 2 cups chicken stock
- 1 tsp salt, plus more to taste

INSTRUCTIONS

1. Cook the bacon in a large skillet until crispy. Remove and crumble.
2. Melt the butter in a large pot over medium heat.
3. Whisk in the flour and cook for 12 minutes.
4. Add the garlic and onion, and cook until softened.
5. Slowly whisk in the milk, half and half, and chicken stock.
6. Add the diced potatoes and bring to a boil.
7. Reduce the heat and let the soup simmer until the potatoes are tender.
8. Stir in the crumbled bacon and season with salt to taste.

Tips

For a thicker soup, you can purée a portion of the soup before adding the bacon.

Garnish with shredded cheddar cheese, chopped green onions, and a dollop of sour cream.

Nutritional Info

Calories: 350

Fat: 15g

Carbs: 30g

Protein: 10g

ITALIAN WEDDING SOUP

Prep: 20 mins | Cook: 30 mins | Serves: 6

INGREDIENTS

- 1 tbsp olive oil
- 1 small onion, grated
- 2 garlic cloves, minced
- 12 cups lowsodium chicken broth
- 1/2 cup grated Parmesan
- 8 oz ground beef
- 8 oz ground pork
- 1/2 cup fresh hearty white bread crumbs
- 1/4 cup chopped fresh Italian parsley
- 1 large egg
- 1 slice fresh white bread, crust trimmed, bread torn into small pieces
- Salt and freshly ground black pepper

INSTRUCTIONS

1. In a large pot, heat the olive oil over medium heat.
2. Add the grated onion and minced garlic, and sauté for 34 minutes until softened.
3. Add the chicken broth and bring to a boil.
4. Reduce the heat and let the soup simmer for 1520 minutes.
5. In a large bowl, combine the ground beef, ground pork, bread crumbs, parsley, egg, and Parmesan. Season with salt and pepper.
6. Roll the meat mixture into small meatballs and add them to the soup.
7. Let the soup simmer for an additional 1015 minutes until the meatballs are cooked through.

Tips

For a heartier soup, you can add cooked pasta or rice.

Garnish with additional grated Parmesan and chopped fresh parsley.

Nutritional Info

Calories: 250

Fat: 12g

Carbs: 20g | Protein: 15g

SNACKS

Fruits and Vegetables

APPLE SLICES WITH PEANUT BUTTER

Prep: 5 mins | Serves: 1

INGREDIENTS:

- 1 medium apple (150g)
- 2 tbsp peanut butter (32g)

INSTRUCTIONS:

1. Wash and slice the apple.
2. Serve with peanut butter for dipping.

Tips: Choose a crunchy apple for extra texture.

Nutritional Info: Calories: 210 | Fat: 16g | Carbs: 18g | Protein: 7g[2]

CELERY STICKS WITH NUT BUTTER

Prep: 5 mins | Serves: 1

INGREDIENTS:

- 2 large celery sticks (80g)
- 2 tbsp almond butter (32g)

INSTRUCTIONS:

1. Wash and cut the celery into sticks.

2. Fill with almond butter.

Tips: Use natural nut butter for a healthier option.

Nutritional Info: Calories: 180 | Fat: 14g | Carbs: 10g | Protein: 6g[2]

CARROTS AND RED PEPPER HUMMUS

Prep: 10 mins | Serves: 2

INGREDIENTS:

- 150g carrots
- 200g red pepper hummus

INSTRUCTIONS:

1. Wash, peel, and cut the carrots.

2. Serve with red pepper hummus.

Tips: Make your own hummus for a lower sodium option.

Nutritional Info: Calories: 120 | Fat: 6g | Carbs: 14g | Protein: 3g[2]

FROZEN GRAPES

Prep: 5 mins | Serves: 1

INGREDIENTS:

- 150g grapes

INSTRUCTIONS:

1. Wash and freeze the grapes.

2. Serve when frozen.

Tips: Try different grape varieties for a mix of flavors.

Nutritional Info: Calories: 100 | Fat: 0g | Carbs: 27g | Protein: 1g[2]

CUCUMBER TOMATO SALAD

Prep: 10 mins | Serves: 2

INGREDIENTS:

- 200g cucumber
- 300g tomatoes
- 30ml olive oil
- 15ml balsamic vinegar

INSTRUCTIONS:

1. Wash and chop the cucumber and tomatoes.

2. Toss with olive oil and balsamic vinegar.

Tips: Add fresh herbs for extra flavor.

Nutritional Info: Calories: 90 | Fat: 7g | Carbs: 7g | Protein: 2g[2]

ROASTED CHICKPEAS

Prep: 5 mins | Cook: 40 mins | Serves: 2

INGREDIENTS:

- 200g canned chickpeas
- 15ml olive oil
- 5g cumin
- 5g paprika

INSTRUCTIONS:

1. Rinse and dry the chickpeas.

2. Toss with olive oil and spices, then roast.

Tips: Experiment with different spice blends.

Nutritional Info: Calories: 220 | Fat: 7g | Carbs: 30g | Protein: 10g[2]

STRAWBERRIES WITH YOGURT DIP

Prep: 5 mins | Serves: 2

INGREDIENTS:

- 300g strawberries
- 200g Greek yogurt
- 5ml honey

INSTRUCTIONS:

1. Wash and hull the strawberries.

2. Mix the yogurt and honey for dipping.

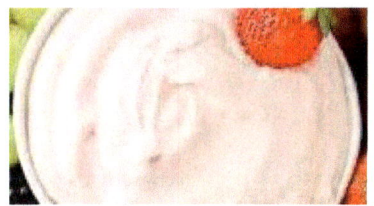

Tips: Use low fat yogurt for a lighter option.

Nutritional Info: Calories: 140 | Fat: 2g | Carbs: 25g | Protein: 7g[2]

CHERRY TOMATO SKEWERS

Prep: 10 mins | Serves: 2

INGREDIENTS:

- 300g cherry tomatoes
- 100g mozzarella balls
- 30ml balsamic glaze

INSTRUCTIONS:

1. Thread the tomatoes and mozzarella onto skewers.

2. Drizzle with balsamic glaze.

Tips: Add fresh basil leaves for extra flavor.

Nutritional Info: Calories: 160 | Fat: 8g | Carbs: 10g | Protein: 12g[2]

FRUIT AND YOGURT BARK

Prep: 10 mins | Cook: 3 hours | Serves: 4

INGREDIENTS:

- 500g Greek yogurt
- 200g mixed berries
- 30ml honey

INSTRUCTIONS:

1. Line a baking tray with parchment paper.

2. Spread the yogurt, then top with berries and honey.

3. Freeze until set, then break into pieces.

Tips: Use any combination of your favorite fruits.

Nutritional Info: Calories: 120 | Fat: 2g | Carbs: 20g | Protein: 8g[2]

BLUEBERRIES WITH TOASTED PECANS

Prep: 5 mins | Serves: 2

INGREDIENTS:

- 300g blueberries
- 50g toasted pecans

INSTRUCTIONS:

1. Wash the blueberries.
2. Serve with toasted pecans.

Tips: Toast the pecans for extra crunch.

Nutritional Info: Calories: 180 | Fat: 12g | Carbs: 20g | Protein: 3g[2]

OTHER SNACKS

AIR POPPED POPCORN

Prep: 5 mins | Cook: 5 mins | Serves: 2

INGREDIENTS:

- 100g popcorn kernels
- 15ml olive oil

INSTRUCTIONS:

1. Pop the kernels using an air popper.

2. Drizzle with olive oil and season to taste.

Tips: Experiment with different seasonings like chili powder or nutritional yeast.

Nutritional Info: Calories: 90 | Fat: 4g | Carbs: 20g | Protein: 3g[2]

WHOLE GRAIN CRACKERS AND CHEESE

Prep: 5 mins | Serves: 2

INGREDIENTS:

- 100g whole grain crackers
- 100g cheddar cheese

INSTRUCTIONS:

1. Arrange the crackers and cheese on a plate.

2. Serve and enjoy.

Tips: Choose a high fiber cracker for added nutrition.

Nutritional Info: Calories: 220 | Fat: 12g | Carbs: 20g | Protein: 8g[2]

COTTAGE CHEESE AND FRUIT

Prep: 5 mins | Serves: 2

INGREDIENTS:

- 200g cottage cheese
- 200g mixed fruit

INSTRUCTIONS:

1. Arrange the cottage cheese and fruit in a bowl.

2. Serve and enjoy.

Tips: Try different fruit combinations like pineapple and mango.

Nutritional Info: Calories: 160 | Fat: 4g | Carbs: 20g | Protein: 12g[2]

HARD BOILED EGGS

Prep: 5 mins | Cook: 10 mins | Serves: 2

INGREDIENTS:

- 4 large eggs (200g)

INSTRUCTIONS:

1. Place the eggs in a saucepan and cover with water.

2. Bring to a boil, then simmer for 810 minutes.

3. Cool in ice water, then peel and enjoy.

Tips: Add a pinch of salt to the water for easier peeling.

Nutritional Info: Calories: 140 | Fat: 10g | Carbs: 1g | Protein: 12g[2]

PROTEIN BARS

INGREDIENTS:

- 200g rolled oats
- 100g protein powder
- 100g almond butter
- 100ml almond milk
- 50g honey

INSTRUCTIONS:

1. Mix all **INGREDIENTS** in a bowl.

2. Press into a lined baking dish and chill.

Tips: Customize with your favorite protein powder flavor.

Nutritional Info: Calories: 250 | Fat: 8g | Carbs: 30g | Protein: 15g[2]

PROTEIN BALLS 4 WAYS

INGREDIENTS:

- 200g dates
- 100g rolled oats
- 100g nut butter
- 50g chia seeds
- 50g shredded coconut

INSTRUCTIONS:

1. Blend dates and oats in a food processor.

2. Add nut butter and chia seeds, then roll into balls.

Tips: Try different coatings like cocoa powder or crushed nuts.

Nutritional Info: Calories: 180 | Fat: 6g | Carbs: 25g | Protein: 8g[2]

FRUIT AND NUT TRAIL MIX

INGREDIENTS:

- 100g almonds
- 100g walnuts
- 100g dried cranberries
- 100g dark chocolate chips

INSTRUCTIONS:

1. Mix all ingredients in a bowl.

2. Portion into snack sized bags for easy grab and go.

Tips: Choose unsweetened dried fruit for a lower sugar option.

Nutritional Info: Calories: 220 | Fat: 18g | Carbs: 15g | Protein: 6g[2]

PUMPKIN SEEDS

Prep: 5 mins | Cook: 10 mins | Serves: 2

INGREDIENTS:

- 100g pumpkin seeds
- 5g olive oil
- 2g salt

INSTRUCTIONS:

1. Toss the pumpkin seeds with olive oil and salt.

2. Roast in the oven until golden.

Tips: Add your favorite spices for extra flavor.

Nutritional Info: Calories: 180 | Fat: 15g | Carbs: 4g | Protein: 10g[2]

ROASTED CHICKPEAS

Prep: 5 mins | Cook: 40 mins | Serves: 2

INGREDIENTS:

- 200g canned chickpeas
- 15ml olive oil
- 5g cumin
- 5g paprika

INSTRUCTIONS:

1. Rinse and dry the chickpeas.

2. Toss with olive oil and spices, then roast.

Tips: Experiment with different spice blends.

Nutritional Info: Calories: 220 | Fat: 7g | Carbs: 30g | Protein: 10g[2]

EDAMAME HUMMUS

Prep: 10 mins | Serves: 4

INGREDIENTS:

- 300g shelled edamame
- 30ml olive oil
- 15ml lemon juice
- 5g garlic

INSTRUCTIONS:

1. Blend all ingredients in a food processor until smooth.
2. Serve with your favorite dippers.

Tips: Try adding fresh herbs like cilantro or mint. **Nutritional Info:** Calories: 160 | Fat: 10g | Carbs: 10g | Protein: 8g[2]

DINNER

BAKED CHICKEN PARMESAN

Prep: 15 mins | Cook: 25 mins | Serves: 4

INGREDIENTS:

- 4 boneless, skinless chicken breasts (about 600g | 1.5 lbs)
- 150g | 1 1/2 cups whole wheat breadcrumbs
- 50g | 1/2 cup grated Parmesan cheese
- 2 large eggs
- 400g | 2 cups tomato sauce
- 200g | 2 cups partskim mozzarella, shredded
- Fresh basil leaves for garnish

INSTRUCTIONS:

1. Preheat the oven to 200°C (180°C fan) | 400°F.
2. In a shallow dish, combine breadcrumbs and Parmesan.
3. In another dish, whisk eggs.
4. Dip each chicken breast into the egg, then coat with breadcrumb mixture, pressing gently.
5. Place chicken on a baking sheet and bake for 20 minutes.
6. Spoon tomato sauce over each breast, top with mozzarella, and bake for an additional 5 minutes or until cheese melts.
7. Garnish with fresh basil and serve.

Tips: For extra crispiness, spray the chicken with cooking spray before baking.

Nutritional Info:

Calories: 320 | Fat: 10g | Carbs: 20g | Protein: 35g

CHICKEN FAJITAS

Prep: 20 mins | Cook: 15 mins | Serves: 4

INGREDIENTS:

- 500g | 1 lb chicken breasts, thinly sliced
- 2 bell peppers, sliced
- 1 large onion, sliced
- 3 tbsp olive oil
- 2 tsp ground cumin
- 2 tsp chili powder
- 1 tsp garlic powder
- 1 tsp onion powder
- 1/2 tsp cayenne pepper
- 8 whole wheat tortillas

INSTRUCTIONS:

1. In a bowl, mix chicken, peppers, onions, and olive oil.
2. In another bowl, combine cumin, chili powder, garlic powder, onion powder, and cayenne.
3. Sprinkle the spice mix over the chicken and vegetables, tossing to coat.
4. Heat a large skillet over mediumhigh heat and cook the chicken mixture for 68 minutes.
5. Warm tortillas in the oven or on the stovetop.
6. Serve the chicken mixture in tortillas.

Tips: Squeeze lime juice for extra flavor.

Nutritional Info:

Calories: 380 | Fat: 15g | Carbs: 35g | Protein: 25g

LEMON GARLIC CHICKEN

Prep: 10 mins | Cook: 20 mins | Serves: 4

INGREDIENTS:

- 4 boneless, skinless chicken breasts (about 600g | 1.5 lbs)
- 3 tbsp olive oil
- 4 cloves garlic, minced
- Zest and juice of 2 lemons
- 1 tsp dried oregano
- Salt and pepper to taste
- Fresh parsley for garnish

INSTRUCTIONS:

1. Season chicken with salt, pepper, and oregano.
2. In a pan, heat olive oil over medium heat.
3. Cook chicken for 67 minutes per side until golden brown.
4. Add garlic, lemon zest, and lemon juice to the pan,

cooking for an additional 34 minutes.

5. Garnish with fresh parsley and serve.

Tips: Marinate chicken for extra flavor.

Nutritional Info:

Calories: 280 | Fat: 12g | Carbs: 2g | Protein: 35g

CHICKEN PICCATA

Prep: 15 mins | Cook: 15 mins | Serves: 4

INGREDIENTS:

- 4 boneless, skinless chicken breasts (about 600g | 1.5 lbs)
- 100g | 1 cup whole wheat flour
- Salt and pepper to taste
- 3 tbsp olive oil
- 2 cloves garlic, minced
- 250ml | 1 cup lowsodium chicken broth
- Juice of 2 lemons
- 2 tbsp capers, drained
- Fresh parsley for garnish

INSTRUCTIONS:

1. Season chicken with salt and pepper, then dredge in flour.
2. Heat olive oil in a pan over mediumhigh heat.
3. Cook chicken for 45 minutes per side until golden brown.
4. Remove chicken and add garlic to the pan, cooking for 1 minute.
5. Pour in chicken broth, lemon juice, and capers, simmering for 5 minutes.
6. Return chicken to the pan to heat through.
7. Garnish with fresh parsley and serve.

Tips: Use whole wheat flour for a nuttier flavor.

Nutritional Info: Calories: 320 | Fat: 12g | Carbs: 20g | Protein: 30g

CHICKEN TIKKA MASALA

Prep: 20 mins | Cook: 25 mins | Serves: 4

INGREDIENTS:

- 500g | 1 lb chicken thighs, diced
- 1 onion, finely chopped
- 3 cloves garlic, minced
- 2 tsp ground cumin
- 2 tsp paprika
- 1 tsp ground coriander
- 1 tsp turmeric
- 400g | 1 3/4 cups chopped tomatoes
- 150ml | 2/3 cup lowfat yogurt
- Fresh cilantro for garnish

INSTRUCTIONS:

1. In a pan, cook chicken until browned. Remove and set aside.
2. In the same pan, sauté onions and garlic until softened.
3. Add cumin, paprika, coriander, and turmeric, cooking for 2 minutes.
4. Stir in chopped tomatoes and simmer for 10 minutes.
5. Add yogurt and cooked chicken, simmering for an additional 5 minutes.
6. Garnish with fresh cilantro and serve over brown rice.

Tips: Adjust spice levels to taste.

Nutritional Info:

Calories: 290 | Fat: 10g | Carbs: 15g | Protein: 30g

ORANGE CHICKEN

Prep: 15 mins | Cook: 20 mins | Serves: 4

INGREDIENTS:

- 500g | 1 lb boneless, skinless chicken thighs, diced
- 2 tbsp cornstarch
- 2 tbsp soy sauce
- 250ml | 1 cup fresh orange juice
- Zest of 1 orange
- 3 tbsp honey
- 1 tbsp rice vinegar
- 2 tsp ginger, grated
- 2 cloves garlic, minced
- 2 tbsp vegetable oil

INSTRUCTIONS:

1. Toss chicken in cornstarch and soy sauce until coated.
2. Heat oil in a pan over mediumhigh heat.
3. Cook chicken until browned, about 5 minutes.

4. In a bowl, mix orange juice, zest, honey, rice vinegar, ginger, and garlic.
5. Pour the orange mixture over the chicken, simmering for 10 minutes.
6. Serve over brown rice.

Tips: Add a pinch of red pepper flakes for heat.

Nutritional Info:

Calories: 310 | Fat: 8g | Carbs: 40g | Protein: 20g

CHICKEN CACCIATORE

Prep: 20 mins | Cook: 30 mins | Serves: 4

INGREDIENTS:

- 4 chicken thighs, bonein and skinon (about 800g | 1.75 lbs)
- 2 tbsp olive oil
- 1 onion, sliced
- 2 bell peppers, sliced
- 2 cloves garlic, minced
- 400g | 1 3/4 cups crushed tomatoes
- 150ml | 2/3 cup red wine
- 1 tsp dried oregano
- 1 tsp dried basil
- Salt and pepper to taste
- Fresh parsley for garnish

INSTRUCTIONS:

1. Season chicken with salt and pepper.
2. In a large skillet, heat olive oil over mediumhigh heat.
3. Brown chicken on both sides, then remove and set aside.
4. In the same pan, sauté onions, peppers, and garlic until softened.
5. Pour in crushed tomatoes, red wine, oregano, and basil, stirring well.
6. Return chicken to the pan, cover, and simmer for 20 minutes.
7. Garnish with fresh parsley before serving.

Tips: Use boneless, skinless chicken thighs for a leaner option.

Nutritional Info:

Calories: 350 | Fat: 15g | Carbs: 15g | Protein: 30g

BALSAMIC CHICKEN

Prep: 10 mins | Cook: 25 mins | Serves: 4

INGREDIENTS:

- 4 boneless, skinless chicken breasts (about 600g | 1.5 lbs)
- 3 tbsp balsamic vinegar
- 2 tbsp olive oil
- 2 cloves garlic, minced
- 1 tsp dried thyme
- Salt and pepper to taste
- 200g | 1 cup cherry tomatoes, halved
- Fresh basil for garnish

INSTRUCTIONS:

1. Season chicken with salt, pepper, and dried thyme.
2. In a bowl, mix balsamic vinegar and olive oil.
3. Marinate chicken in the balsamic mixture for 10 minutes.
4. In a pan, cook chicken for 67 minutes per side.
5. Add garlic and cherry tomatoes, cooking for an additional 5 minutes.
6. Garnish with fresh basil and serve.

Tips: Drizzle extra balsamic before serving.

Nutritional Info:

Calories: 280 | Fat: 10g | Carbs: 10g | Protein: 35g

CHICKEN FRIED RICE

Prep: 15 mins | Cook: 20 mins | Serves: 4

INGREDIENTS:

- 300g | 1 1/2 cups brown rice, cooked
- 2 chicken breasts, cooked and diced (about 400g | 0.9 lbs)
- 2 tbsp vegetable oil
- 2 carrots, diced
- 100g | 1/2 cup peas
- 2 eggs, beaten
- 3 tbsp lowsodium soy sauce
- 1 tsp sesame oil
- 2 spring onions, sliced

INSTRUCTIONS:

1. In a wok or large pan, heat vegetable oil over mediumhigh heat.
2. Add carrots and peas, stirfrying for 3 minutes.
3. Push vegetables to one side, add beaten eggs, and scramble.
4. Mix in cooked rice and chicken, stirring well.
5. Pour soy sauce and sesame oil over the mixture, stirring to combine.

6. Garnish with sliced spring onions and serve.

Tips: Use leftover rice for better texture.

Nutritional Info:

Calories: 320 | Fat: 8g | Carbs: 40g | Protein: 20g

BUFFALO CHICKEN LETTUCE WRAPS

Prep: 15 mins | Cook: 15 mins | Serves: 4

INGREDIENTS:

- 500g | 1 lb ground chicken
- 1 tbsp olive oil
- 1/2 cup hot sauce
- 1 tsp garlic powder
- 1 tsp onion powder
- 1 tsp dried parsley
- Salt and pepper to taste
- 8 large lettuce leaves
- Celery sticks for serving

INSTRUCTIONS:

1. In a pan, heat olive oil over medium high heat.
2. Add ground chicken and cook until browned.
3. Stir in hot sauce, garlic powder, onion powder, dried parsley, salt, and pepper.
4. Simmer for 5 minutes until heated through.
5. Spoon the buffalo chicken mixture into lettuce leaves.
6. Serve with celery sticks on the side.

Tips: Add a dollop of Greek yogurt for a cooling effect.

Nutritional Info:

Calories: 260 | Fat: 15g | Carbs: 2g | Protein: 30g

Seafood

LEMON GARLIC SHRIMP

Prep: 10 mins | Cook: 10 mins | Serves: 4

INGREDIENTS:

- 500g | 1 lb large shrimp, peeled and deveined
- 3 tbsp olive oil
- 4 cloves garlic, minced
- Zest and juice of 2 lemons
- 1 tsp dried oregano
- Salt and pepper to taste
- Fresh parsley for garnish

INSTRUCTIONS:

1. In a pan, heat olive oil over mediumhigh heat.
2. Add shrimp, garlic, lemon zest, lemon juice, and oregano.
3. Cook for 34 minutes until shrimp are pink and opaque.
4. Season with salt and pepper.
5. Garnish with fresh parsley and serve.

Tips: Serve over whole wheat pasta for a complete meal.

Nutritional Info:

Calories: 180 | Fat: 10g | Carbs: 2g | Protein: 20g

CAJUN SALMON

Prep: 15 mins | Cook: 15 mins | Serves: 4

INGREDIENTS:

- 4 salmon fillets (about 600g | 1.5 lbs)
- 2 tbsp olive oil
- 1 tbsp Cajun seasoning
- 1 tsp garlic powder
- 1 tsp onion powder
- 1 tsp paprika
- 1/2 tsp dried thyme
- Lemon wedges for serving

INSTRUCTIONS:

1. Preheat the oven to 200°C (180°C fan) | 400°F.
2. Place salmon fillets on a baking sheet.
3. In a bowl, mix olive oil, Cajun seasoning, garlic powder, onion powder, paprika, and thyme.
4. Brush the spice mixture over each fillet.
5. Bake for 1215 minutes until salmon flakes easily.
6. Serve with lemon wedges.

Tips: Adjust Cajun seasoning to suit your spice preference.

Nutritional Info:

Calories: 280 | Fat: 15g | Carbs: 1g | Protein: 30g

TUNA SALAD STUFFED TOMATOES

Prep: 15 mins | Cook: 0 mins | Serves: 4

INGREDIENTS:

- 4 large tomatoes
- 200g | 1 cup canned tuna, drained
- 1/2 cup cucumber, diced
- 1/4 cup red onion, finely chopped
- 2 tbsp mayonnaise
- 1 tbsp Dijon mustard
- Salt and pepper to taste
- Fresh parsley for garnish

INSTRUCTIONS:

1. Cut the tops off the tomatoes and scoop out the insides.
2. In a bowl, mix tuna, cucumber, red onion, mayonnaise, and Dijon mustard.
3. Season with salt and pepper to taste.
4. Spoon the tuna salad into the hollowedout tomatoes.
5. Garnish with fresh parsley and serve.

Tips: Serve on a bed of mixed greens for extra freshness.

Nutritional Info:

Calories: 180 | Fat: 10g | Carbs: 10g | Protein: 15g

CRAB CAKES

Prep: 20 mins | Cook: 10 mins | Serves: 4

INGREDIENTS:

- 250g | 1 cup lump crab meat
- 1/4 cup whole wheat breadcrumbs
- 1/4 cup mayonnaise
- 1 egg, beaten
- 2 tbsp fresh parsley, chopped
- 1 tsp Dijon mustard
- 1/2 tsp Worcestershire sauce
- 1/4 tsp Old Bay seasoning
- 2 tbsp olive oil

INSTRUCTIONS:

1. In a bowl, combine crab meat, breadcrumbs, mayonnaise, egg, parsley, Dijon mustard, Worcestershire sauce, and Old Bay seasoning.
2. Form the mixture into small patties.
3. Heat olive oil in a pan over medium heat.
4. Cook crab cakes for 34 minutes per side until golden brown.
5. Serve with a squeeze of lemon.

Tips: Use whole wheat breadcrumbs for added fiber.

Nutritional Info:

Calories: 220 | Fat: 15g | Carbs: 5g | Protein: 15g

BLACKENED TILAPIA

Prep: 10 mins | Cook: 10 mins | Serves: 4

INGREDIENTS:

- 4 tilapia fillets (about 600g | 1.5 lbs)
- 2 tsp paprika
- 1 tsp onion powder
- 1 tsp garlic powder
- 1 tsp dried thyme
- 1/2 tsp cayenne pepper
- 2 tbsp olive oil
- Lemon wedges for serving

INSTRUCTIONS:

1. In a small bowl, mix paprika, onion powder, garlic powder, thyme, and cayenne pepper.
2. Rub the spice mixture over both sides of each tilapia fillet.
3. Heat olive oil in a pan over medium high heat.
4. Cook tilapia for 34 minutes per side until blackened.

5. Serve with lemon wedges.

Tips: Adjust cayenne pepper to control spiciness.

Nutritional Info:

Calories: 200 | Fat: 8g | Carbs: 1g | Protein: 30g

BAKED COD

Prep: 15 mins | Cook: 20 mins | Serves: 4

INGREDIENTS:

- 4 cod fillets (about 600g | 1.5 lbs)
- 3 tbsp olive oil
- 2 cloves garlic, minced
- 1 tsp dried oregano
- 1 tsp dried basil
- 1/2 tsp onion powder
- Salt and pepper to taste
- Lemon wedges for serving

INSTRUCTIONS:

1. Preheat the oven to 200°C (180°C fan) | 400°F.
2. Place cod fillets on a baking sheet.
3. In a bowl, mix olive oil, garlic, oregano, basil, onion powder, salt, and pepper.
4. Brush the mixture over each fillet.

5. Bake for 1520 minutes until cod flakes easily.
6. Serve with lemon wedges.

Tips: Use fresh herbs for a burst of flavor.

Nutritional Info:

Calories: 250 | Fat: 12g | Carbs: 1g | Protein: 30g

SHRIMP AND VEGETABLE KEBABS

Prep: 15 mins | Cook: 10 mins | Serves: 4

INGREDIENTS:

- 500g | 1 lb large shrimp, peeled and deveined
- 2 bell peppers, cut into chunks
- 1 zucchini, sliced
- 1 red onion, sliced
- 3 tbsp olive oil
- 1 tsp smoked paprika
- 1 tsp garlic powder
- 1 tsp dried thyme
- Salt and pepper to taste
- Lemon wedges for serving

INSTRUCTIONS:

1. In a bowl, toss shrimp, bell peppers, zucchini, and red onion with olive oil, paprika, garlic powder, thyme, salt, and pepper.
2. Thread the shrimp and vegetables onto skewers.
3. Grill or broil for 34 minutes per side until shrimp are pink and vegetables are tender.
4. Serve with lemon wedges.

Tips: Soak wooden skewers in water before grilling to prevent burning.

Nutritional Info:

Calories: 230 | Fat: 12g | Carbs: 10g | Protein: 20g

SALMON BURGERS

Prep: 15 mins | Cook: 10 mins | Serves: 4

INGREDIENTS:

- 500g | 1 lb salmon fillet, skinless and boneless
- 1/4 cup whole wheat breadcrumbs
- 1 egg, beaten
- 2 green onions, finely chopped
- 1 tbsp Dijon mustard
- 1 tsp lemon zest
- 1/2 tsp dried dill
- Salt and pepper to taste
- 4 whole wheat burger buns

INSTRUCTIONS:

1. In a food processor, pulse salmon until coarsely chopped.
2. In a bowl, combine salmon, breadcrumbs, egg, green onions, Dijon mustard, lemon zest, dill, salt, and pepper.
3. Form the mixture into 4 patties.
4. Heat a grill or skillet over medium high heat.
5. Cook salmon burgers for 45 minutes per side until cooked through.

6. Serve on whole wheat buns.

Tips: Top with Greek yogurt and cucumber for a refreshing twist.

Nutritional Info:

Calories: 300 | Fat: 15g | Carbs: 20g | Protein: 25g

TUNA NOODLE CASSEROLE

Prep: 20 mins | Cook: 25 mins | Serves: 4

INGREDIENTS:

- 250g | 3 cups whole wheat egg noodles, cooked
- 200g | 1 cup canned tuna, drained
- 1 cup frozen peas, thawed
- 1/2 cup carrots, diced
- 1/4 cup whole wheat flour
- 2 cups skim milk
- 1 cup lowfat cheddar cheese, shredded
- 1 tsp Dijon mustard
- Salt and pepper to taste
- 2 tbsp whole wheat breadcrumbs

INSTRUCTIONS:

1. Preheat the oven to 200°C (180°C fan) | 400°F.
2. In a large bowl, combine cooked noodles, tuna, peas, and carrots.
3. In a saucepan, whisk flour into milk over medium heat until thickened.
4. Stir in cheddar cheese, Dijon mustard, salt, and pepper until cheese melts.
5. Pour the cheese sauce over the noodle mixture and toss to coat.
6. Transfer to a baking dish, sprinkle with breadcrumbs, and bake for 2025 minutes.
7. Serve hot.

Tips: Add a pinch of nutmeg for depth of flavor.

Nutritional Info:

Calories: 320 | Fat: 8g | Carbs: 40g | Protein: 20g

COCONUT SHRIMP

Prep: 20 mins | Cook: 15 mins | Serves: 4

INGREDIENTS:

- 500g | 1 lb large shrimp, peeled and deveined
- 1/2 cup whole wheat flour
- 2 eggs, beaten
- 1 cup unsweetened shredded coconut
- 1 cup whole wheat breadcrumbs
- 1 tsp garlic powder
- 1/2 tsp onion powder
- Salt and pepper to taste
- Sweet chili sauce for dipping

INSTRUCTIONS:

1. Preheat the oven to 200°C (180°C fan) | 400°F.
2. Set up a breading station with three bowls: one with flour, one with beaten eggs, and one with a mixture of shredded coconut, breadcrumbs, garlic powder, onion powder, salt, and pepper.
3. Dredge each shrimp in flour, dip in beaten eggs, then coat with the coconut mixture.
4. Place the coated shrimp on a baking sheet.
5. Bake for 1215 minutes until golden brown.
6. Serve with sweet chili sauce for dipping.

Tips: Use large shrimp for better coconut coverage.

Nutritional Info:

Calories: 250 | Fat: 10g | Carbs: 30g | Protein: 15g

MEATLESS MAINS

EGGPLANT PARMESAN

Prep: 30 mins | Cook: 40 mins | Serves: 4

INGREDIENTS:

- 1 large eggplant, sliced
- 2 cups whole wheat breadcrumbs
- 1 cup grated Parmesan cheese
- 2 eggs, beaten
- 500g | 2 cups tomato sauce
- 200g | 2 cups partskim mozzarella, shredded
- Fresh basil leaves for garnish

INSTRUCTIONS:

1. Preheat the oven to 200°C (180°C fan) | 400°F.
2. Dip eggplant slices in beaten eggs, then coat with a mixture of breadcrumbs and Parmesan.
3. Place the coated eggplant on a baking sheet and bake for 20 minutes.
4. In a baking dish, layer tomato sauce, baked eggplant, and mozzarella.
5. Repeat the layers, finishing with mozzarella on top.
6. Bake for an additional 20 minutes until bubbly and golden.
7. Garnish with fresh basil and serve.

Tips: Salting the eggplant before baking removes excess moisture.

Nutritional Info:

Calories: 280 | Fat: 10g | Carbs: 30g | Protein: 15g

BLACK BEAN VEGGIE BURGERS

Prep: 20 mins | Cook: 10 mins | Serves: 4

INGREDIENTS:

- 400g | 2 cups canned black beans, drained and rinsed
- 1 cup breadcrumbs
- 1/2 cup red bell pepper, diced
- 1/2 cup corn kernels
- 1/4 cup red onion, finely chopped
- 2 cloves garlic, minced
- 1 tsp cumin
- 1 tsp chili powder
- Salt and pepper to taste
- 4 whole wheat burger buns
- Lettuce, tomato, and avocado for topping

Tips: Refrigerate patties for 30 minutes before cooking for better consistency.

Nutritional Info:

Calories: 320 | Fat: 8g | Carbs: 50g | Protein: 15g

INSTRUCTIONS:

1. In a food processor, pulse black beans until partially mashed.
2. In a bowl, combine mashed black beans, breadcrumbs, red bell pepper, corn, red onion, garlic, cumin, chili powder, salt, and pepper.
3. Form the mixture into 4 patties.
4. Heat a grill or skillet over mediumhigh heat.
5. Cook veggie burgers for 45 minutes per side until golden brown.
6. Serve on whole wheat buns with lettuce, tomato, and avocado.

QUINOA STUFFED PEPPERS

Prep: 20 mins | Cook: 25 mins | Serves: 4

INGREDIENTS:

- 4 bell peppers, halved and seeds removed
- 1 cup quinoa, cooked
- 400g | 2 cups black beans, cooked and drained
- 1 cup corn kernels
- 1 cup cherry tomatoes, halved
- 1/2 cup red onion, finely chopped
- 1 tsp cumin
- 1 tsp chili powder
- Salt and pepper to taste
- 200g | 1 cup tomato sauce
- 100g | 1 cup partskim mozzarella, shredded
- Fresh cilantro for garnish

INSTRUCTIONS:

1. Preheat the oven to 200°C (180°C fan) | 400°F.
2. In a bowl, combine cooked quinoa, black beans, corn, cherry tomatoes, red onion, cumin, chili powder, salt, and pepper.
3. Spoon the quinoa mixture into halved bell peppers.
4. Pour tomato sauce over the stuffed peppers.
5. Top with mozzarella and bake for 25 minutes until cheese is melted and bubbly.

6. Garnish with fresh cilantro and serve.

Tips: Add a pinch of smoked paprika for extra flavor.

Nutritional Info:

Calories: 280 | Fat: 8g | Carbs: 40g | Protein: 15g

LENTIL SLOPPY JOES

Prep: 15 mins | Cook: 25 mins | Serves: 4

INGREDIENTS:

- 1 cup green lentils, cooked
- 1 tbsp olive oil
- 1 onion, finely chopped
- 2 cloves garlic, minced
- 1 bell pepper, diced
- 1 carrot, grated
- 400g | 2 cups crushed tomatoes
- 2 tbsp tomato paste
- 2 tbsp Worcestershire sauce
- 1 tbsp maple syrup
- 1 tsp Dijon mustard
- 1 tsp ground cumin
- 1/2 tsp smoked paprika
- Salt and pepper to taste
- 4 whole wheat burger buns

INSTRUCTIONS:

1. In a pan, heat olive oil over medium heat.
2. Add chopped onion and minced garlic, sautéing until softened.
3. Stir in diced bell pepper and grated carrot, cooking for an additional 34 minutes.
4. Add cooked lentils, crushed tomatoes, tomato paste, Worcestershire sauce, maple syrup, Dijon mustard, ground cumin, smoked paprika, salt, and pepper to the pan, stirring well.
5. Simmer for 1520 minutes until the mixture thickens.
6. Season with additional salt and pepper to taste.
7. Serve the lentil Sloppy Joes on whole wheat buns.

Tips: Toast the buns for added texture.

Nutritional Info:

Calories: 290 | Fat: 5g | Carbs: 50g | Protein: 15g

VEGGIE FAJITAS

Prep: 20 mins | Cook: 15 mins | Serves: 4

INGREDIENTS:

- 2 bell peppers, sliced
- 1 onion, sliced
- 1 zucchini, sliced
- 1 cup cherry tomatoes, halved
- 2 tbsp olive oil
- 2 tsp ground cumin
- 2 tsp chili powder
- 1 tsp garlic powder
- 1 tsp onion powder
- 1/2 tsp smoked paprika
- 8 whole wheat tortillas
- Guacamole and salsa for serving

INSTRUCTIONS:

1. In a large skillet, heat olive oil over mediumhigh heat.
2. Add sliced bell peppers, onion, zucchini, and cherry tomatoes to the pan.
3. Sprinkle cumin, chili powder, garlic powder, onion powder, and smoked paprika over the vegetables, tossing to coat.
4. Sauté for 810 minutes until vegetables are tendercrisp.
5. Warm tortillas in the oven or on the stovetop.
6. Serve the fajita mixture in tortillas with guacamole and salsa.

Tips: Customize with your favorite fajita toppings.

Nutritional Info:

Calories: 250 | Fat: 8g | Carbs: 40g | Protein: 10g

PORTOBELLO MUSHROOM STEAKS

Prep: 15 mins | Cook: 15 mins | Serves: 4

INGREDIENTS:

- 4 large portobello mushrooms
- 3 tbsp balsamic vinegar
- 2 tbsp olive oil
- 2 cloves garlic, minced
- 1 tsp dried thyme
- Salt and pepper to taste
- Fresh parsley for garnish

INSTRUCTIONS:

1. Preheat the oven to 200°C (180°C fan) | 400°F.
2. Clean portobello mushrooms and remove the stems.
3. In a bowl, whisk together balsamic vinegar, olive oil, minced garlic, dried thyme, salt, and pepper.
4. Brush the mushroom caps with the balsamic mixture.
5. Place the mushrooms on a baking sheet and roast for 15 minutes.
6. Garnish with fresh parsley before serving.

Tips: Serve mushroom steaks over quinoa for a complete meal.

Nutritional Info:

Calories: 120 | Fat: 8g | Carbs: 10g | Protein: 4g

BROCCOLI RICE CASSEROLE

Prep: 15 mins | Cook: 30 mins | Serves: 4

INGREDIENTS:

- 2 cups broccoli florets
- 200g | 1 cup brown rice, cooked
- 1 cup lowfat cheddar cheese, shredded
- 1/2 cup Greek yogurt
- 2 tbsp whole wheat flour
- 1 cup skim milk
- 1 tsp Dijon mustard
- Salt and pepper to taste
- 2 tbsp whole wheat breadcrumbs

INSTRUCTIONS:

1. Preheat the oven to 200°C (180°C fan) | 400°F.
2. Steam broccoli until tendercrisp.
3. In a large bowl, combine cooked brown rice, steamed broccoli, and shredded cheddar cheese.
4. In a saucepan, whisk together Greek yogurt, whole wheat flour, skim milk, Dijon mustard, salt, and pepper over medium heat until thickened.
5. Pour the yogurt mixture over the broccoli and rice, tossing to coat.
6. Transfer the mixture to a baking dish, sprinkle with

whole wheat breadcrumbs, and bake for 2530 minutes.

7. Serve hot.

Tips: Add cooked chicken for a protein boost.

Nutritional Info:

Calories: 280 | Fat: 8g | Carbs: 40g | Protein: 15g

ZUCCHINI LASAGNA

Prep: 30 mins | Cook: 40 mins | Serves: 4

INGREDIENTS:

- 4 large zucchini, sliced lengthwise
- 500g | 2 cups lean ground turkey
- 1 onion, finely chopped
- 2 cloves garlic, minced
- 400g | 2 cups tomato sauce
- 1 tsp dried oregano
- 1 tsp dried basil
- 250g | 1 cup ricotta cheese
- 1 cup partskim mozzarella, shredded
- Fresh basil for garnish

INSTRUCTIONS:

1. Preheat the oven to 200°C (180°C fan) |
1. 400°F.

2. In a pan, cook ground turkey, onion, and garlic until browned.
3. Stir in tomato sauce, oregano, and basil, simmering for 10 minutes.
4. In a bowl, combine ricotta cheese and shredded mozzarella.
5. In a baking dish, layer zucchini slices, meat sauce, and cheese mixture.
6. Repeat the layers, finishing with cheese on top.
7. Bake for 3040 minutes until bubbly and golden.
8. Garnish with fresh basil and serve.

Tips: Let the lasagna rest for 10 minutes before serving.

Nutritional Info:

Calories: 320 | Fat: 15g | Carbs: 20g | Protein: 25g

SWEET POTATO BLACK BEAN TACOS

Prep: 20 mins | Cook: 25 mins | Serves: 4

INGREDIENTS:

- 2 large sweet potatoes, diced
- 400g | 2 cups canned black beans, drained and rinsed
- 1 tbsp olive oil
- 1 tsp ground cumin
- 1 tsp chili powder
- 1/2 tsp smoked paprika
- Salt and pepper to taste
- 8 whole wheat tortillas
- Cabbage slaw for topping

INSTRUCTIONS:

1. Preheat the oven to 200°C (180°C fan) | 400°F.
2. Toss diced sweet potatoes with olive oil, cumin, chili powder, smoked paprika, salt, and pepper.
3. Roast sweet potatoes on a baking sheet for 2025 minutes until tender.
4. In a pan, warm black beans over medium heat.
5. Warm tortillas in the oven or on the stovetop.
6. Assemble tacos with roasted sweet potatoes, black beans, and cabbage slaw.

Tips: Top with avocado and a squeeze of lime.

Nutritional Info:

Calories: 280 | Fat: 5g | Carbs: 50g | Protein: 10g

VEGGIE POT PIE

Prep: 30 mins | Cook: 30 mins | Serves: 4

INGREDIENTS:

- 2 tbsp olive oil
- 1 onion, finely chopped
- 2 carrots, diced
- 2 potatoes, diced
- 1 cup frozen peas
- 1/4 cup whole wheat flour
- 2 cups vegetable broth
- 1 cup skim milk
- 1 tsp dried thyme
- Salt and pepper to taste
- 1 sheet puff pastry, thawed
- 1 egg, beaten

INSTRUCTIONS:

1. Preheat the oven to 200°C (180°C fan) | 400°F.
2. In a pot, heat olive oil over medium heat.
3. Sauté chopped onion, diced carrots, and potatoes until vegetables are softened.
4. Stir in frozen peas and sprinkle whole wheat flour over the mixture, stirring well.
5. Pour in vegetable broth and skim milk, stirring constantly until the mixture thickens.
6. Season with dried thyme, salt, and pepper to taste.

7. Transfer the veggie mixture to a baking dish.
8. Roll out puff pastry and place it over the filling, trimming any excess.
9. Brush the pastry with beaten egg.
10.   Bake for 2530 minutes until the pastry is golden and the filling is bubbling.
11.   Serve hot.

Tips: Use a mix of your favorite vegetables for variety.

Nutritional Info:

 Calories: 320 | Fat: 15g | Carbs: 40g | Protein: 10g

DESSERTS

Fruits

MIXED BERRY FRUIT SALAD

Prep: 15 mins | Serves: 4

INGREDIENTS:

- 200g (7 oz) strawberries, hulled and halved (1 1/2 cups)
- 150g (5.3 oz) blueberries (1 cup)
- 150g (5.3 oz) raspberries (1 cup)
- 2 tbsp (30ml) honey

INSTRUCTIONS:

1. In a large bowl, combine the strawberries, blueberries, and raspberries.
2. Drizzle honey over the fruit and gently toss to coat.

Tips: Serve chilled. Add a squeeze of fresh lime juice for extra zing.

Nutritional Info: Calories: 80 | Fat: 0.5g | Carbs: 20g | Protein: 1g[1]

BAKED APPLES

Prep: 10 mins | Cook: 30 mins | Serves: 4

INGREDIENTS:

- 4 medium apples, cored
- 40g (3 tbsp) brown sugar
- 1 tsp (5ml) ground cinnamon

INSTRUCTIONS:

1. Preheat the oven to 180°C (350°F).
2. In a small bowl, mix the brown sugar and cinnamon.
3. Place the apples in a baking dish and fill each core with the sugar mixture.
4. Bake for 30 minutes or until tender.

Tips: Serve with a dollop of Greek yogurt and a sprinkle of granola.

Nutritional Info: Calories: 140 | Fat: 0g | Carbs: 37g | Protein: 0g[1]

FRUIT CRUMBLE

Prep: 15 mins | Cook: 40 mins | Serves: 6

INGREDIENTS:

- 500g (4 cups) mixed berries
- 50g (1/4 cup) granulated sugar
- 100g (1 cup) rolled oats
- 60g (1/2 cup) wholemeal flour
- 60ml (1/4 cup) honey
- 60g (1/4 cup) unsalted butter, melted

INSTRUCTIONS:

1. Preheat the oven to 180°C (350°F).
2. In a bowl, toss the mixed berries with granulated sugar and place in a baking dish.
3. In another bowl, combine oats, flour, honey, and melted butter. Sprinkle over the berries.
4. Bake for 40 minutes or until the top is golden and the fruit is bubbling.

Tips: Serve with a scoop of lowfat vanilla ice cream.

Nutritional Info: Calories: 220 | Fat: 6g | Carbs: 40g | Protein: 4g[1]

STRAWBERRY SHORTCAKE

Prep: 20 mins | Cook: 15 mins | Serves: 6

INGREDIENTS:

- 200g (1 2/3 cups) wholemeal flour
- 2 tsp (10ml) baking powder
- 30g (1/4 cup) granulated sugar
- 60g (1/4 cup) unsalted butter, cold and cubed
- 120ml (1/2 cup) lowfat milk
- 500g (4 cups) fresh strawberries, sliced
- 240ml (1 cup) lowfat whipped cream

INSTRUCTIONS:

1. Preheat the oven to 200°C (400°F).
2. In a bowl, whisk together the flour, baking powder, and granulated sugar.
3. Cut in the cold butter until the mixture resembles coarse crumbs.
4. Stir in the milk until a soft dough forms. Drop onto a baking sheet and bake for 15 minutes.
5. To assemble, split the shortcakes, fill with strawberries, and top with

whipped cream.

Tips: Use a heart shaped cutter for a fun twist. Substitute half the strawberries with raspberries.

Nutritional Info: Calories: 180 | Fat: 5g | Carbs: 30g | Protein: 3g[1]

FRUIT PIZZA

Prep: 20 mins | Cook: 15 mins | Serves: 8

INGREDIENTS:

- 200g (1 2/3 cups) wholemeal flour
- 2 tsp (10ml) baking powder
- 30g (1/4 cup) granulated sugar
- 60g (1/4 cup) unsalted butter, cold and cubed
- 120ml (1/2 cup) lowfat milk
- 240g (1 cup) lowfat cream cheese
- 60ml (1/4 cup) honey
- 500g (4 cups) assorted fresh fruit (e.g., kiwi, berries, pineapple)

INSTRUCTIONS:

1. Preheat the oven to 200°C (400°F).
2. In a bowl, whisk together the flour, baking powder, and granulated sugar.
3. Cut in the cold butter until the mixture resembles coarse crumbs.
4. Stir in the milk until a soft dough forms. Press onto a pizza pan and bake for 15 minutes.
5. In another bowl, beat the cream cheese and honey until smooth. Spread over the cooled crust.
6. Arrange the fruit on top. Refrigerate until ready to serve.

Tips: Brush the baked crust with a little apricot jam for extra shine. Get creative with the fruit arrangement.

Nutritional Info: Calories: 220 | Fat: 6g | Carbs: 40g | Protein: 4g[1]

FRUIT AND YOGURT BARS

Prep: 20 mins | Cook: 6 hours | Serves: 12

INGREDIENTS:

- 500g (2 cups) lowfat Greek yogurt
- 200g (1 1/2 cups) mixed berries
- 60ml (1/4 cup) honey
- 100g (1 cup) granola

INSTRUCTIONS:

1. Line a 20x20cm (8x8inch) baking dish with parchment paper.
2. In a bowl, mix the yogurt and honey. Spread half of the mixture into the prepared dish.
3. Sprinkle with half of the granola and half of the berries. Repeat layers.
4. Freeze for at least 6 hours or until firm. Cut into bars.

Tips: Use any combination of your favorite fruits. Store bars in an airtight container in the freezer.

Nutritional Info: Calories: 120 | Fat: 2g | Carbs: 20g | Protein: 5g[1]

TROPICAL FRUIT BOWLS

Prep: 15 mins | Serves: 4

INGREDIENTS:

- 2 large mangoes, peeled and diced
- 2 large kiwifruit, peeled and diced
- 1 small pineapple, peeled and diced
- 1 large papaya, peeled, seeded, and diced
- 1 lime, juiced
- 30ml (2 tbsp) honey

INSTRUCTIONS:

1. In a large bowl, combine the mangoes, kiwifruit, pineapple, and papaya.
2. Drizzle with lime juice and honey. Toss gently to coat.

Tips: Serve in hollowed out pineapple halves for a fun presentation. Top with a sprinkle of toasted coconut.

Nutritional Info: Calories: 150 | Fat: 1g | Carbs: 40g | Protein: 2g[1]

FRUIT NACHOS

Prep: 10 mins | Cook: 10 mins | Serves: 4

Nutritional Info: Calories: 180 | Fat: 5g | Carbs: 30g | Protein: 3g[1]

INGREDIENTS:

- 2 whole wheat pitas
- 30ml (2 tbsp) coconut oil, melted
- 15ml (1 tbsp) granulated sugar
- 5ml (1 tsp) ground cinnamon
- 200g (1 2/3 cups) mixed berries
- 120g (1 cup) lowfat vanilla yogurt

INSTRUCTIONS:

1. Preheat the oven to 180°C (350°F).
2. Brush the pitas with melted coconut oil and sprinkle with sugar and cinnamon.
3. Cut each pita into 8 wedges and place on a baking sheet. Bake for 10 minutes or until crisp.
4. Arrange the baked pita chips on a serving platter. Top with mixed berries and dollops of vanilla yogurt.

Tips: Drizzle with a little honey for extra sweetness. Try using different fruits like sliced bananas or peaches.

FRUIT CREPES

Prep: 10 mins | Cook: 20 mins | Serves: 4

INGREDIENTS:

- 125g (1 cup) whole meal flour
- 250ml (1 cup) low fat milk
- 2 large eggs
- 15ml (1 tbsp) honey
- 5ml (1 tsp) vanilla extract
- 200g (1 2/3 cups) mixed berries
- 120ml (1/2 cup) low fat Greek yogurt

INSTRUCTIONS:

1. In a blender, combine the flour, milk, eggs, honey, and vanilla. Blend until smooth.
2. Heat a nonstick pan over medium heat and lightly grease with cooking spray.
3. Pour 60ml (1/4 cup) of batter into the pan, swirling to coat the bottom. Cook for 2 minutes, then flip and cook for an additional 1 minute.
4. Repeat with the remaining batter. Serve each crepe filled with mixed berries and a dollop of Greek yogurt.

Tips: Dust with a little icing sugar before serving. Add a squeeze of lemon juice to the berries for a zesty kick.

Nutritional Info: Calories: 200 | Fat: 3g | Carbs: 35g | Protein: 8g[1]

FRUIT KEBABS 5 WAYS

Prep: 20 mins | Cook: 5 mins | Serves: 4

INGREDIENTS:

- 200g (1 2/3 cups) pineapple, cut into chunks
- 200g (1 2/3 cups) strawberries, hulled
- 200g (1 2/3 cups) kiwifruit, peeled and cut into chunks
- 200g (1 2/3 cups) mango, cut into chunks
- 200g (1 2/3 cups) banana, cut into chunks
- 60ml (1/4 cup) honey

INSTRUCTIONS:

1. Preheat a grill or barbecue to mediumhigh heat.
2. Thread the fruit onto skewers, alternating the varieties.
3. Grill for 23 minutes on each side or until lightly charred.
4. Drizzle with honey before serving.

Tips: Soak wooden skewers in water for 30 minutes before threading to prevent burning. Serve with a side of lowfat vanilla yogurt for dipping.

Nutritional Info: Calories: 160 | Fat: 1g | Carbs: 40g | Protein: 2g[1]

Other Desserts

PEANUT BUTTER ENERGY BITES

Prep: 15 mins | Cook: 0 mins | Serves: 12

INGREDIENTS:

- 120g (1 1/4 cups) rolled oats
- 60g (1/2 cup) ground flaxseed
- 120g (1/2 cup) natural peanut butter
- 60ml (1/4 cup) honey
- 60g (1/2 cup) dark chocolate chips

INSTRUCTIONS:

1. In a bowl, mix together the oats, flaxseed, peanut butter, and honey until well combined.
2. Fold in the chocolate chips. Roll the mixture into 12 balls and refrigerate until firm.

Tips: Add a scoop of vanilla protein powder for an extra protein boost. Store energy bites in an airtight container in the fridge for up to a week.

Nutritional Info: Calories: 150 | Fat: 7g | Carbs: 20g | Protein: 5g[1]

GREEK YOGURT PUDDING

Prep: 5 mins | Cook: 0 mins | Serves: 4

INGREDIENTS:

- 500g (2 cups) lowfat Greek yogurt
- 60ml (1/4 cup) honey
- 5ml (1 tsp) vanilla extract
- 60g (1/2 cup) mixed berries

INSTRUCTIONS:

1. In a bowl, whisk together the yogurt, honey, and vanilla until smooth.
2. Divide the mixture among 4 serving glasses and top with mixed berries.

Tips: Chill the pudding for an hour before serving for a firmer texture. Sprinkle with a few chopped nuts for added crunch.

Nutritional Info: Calories: 120 | Fat: 2g | Carbs: 15g | Protein: 10g[1]

PUMPKIN PROTEIN MOUSSE

Prep: 10 mins | Cook: 0 mins | Serves: 4

INGREDIENTS:

- 400g (1 3/4 cups) canned pumpkin puree
- 240ml (1 cup) unsweetened almond milk
- 60g (1/4 cup) honey
- 30g (1/4 cup) vanilla protein powder
- 5ml (1 tsp) pumpkin pie spice

INSTRUCTIONS:

1. In a blender, combine the pumpkin puree, almond milk, honey, protein powder, and pumpkin pie spice. Blend until smooth.
2. Divide the mousse among 4 serving glasses. Refrigerate for at least 2 hours before serving.

Tips: Top with a dollop of Greek yogurt and a sprinkle of cinnamon before serving. This mousse can be made a day in advance.

Nutritional Info: Calories: 110 | Fat: 1g | Carbs: 20g | Protein: 7g[1]

DARK CHOCOLATE AVOCADO MOUSSE

Prep: 10 mins | Cook: 0 mins | Serves: 4

INGREDIENTS:

- 2 ripe avocados, pitted and peeled
- 60g (1/2 cup) unsweetened cocoa powder
- 120ml (1/2 cup) unsweetened almond milk
- 60ml (1/4 cup) honey
- 5ml (1 tsp) vanilla extract

INSTRUCTIONS:

1. In a food processor, combine the avocados, cocoa powder, almond milk, honey, and vanilla extract. Blend until creamy.
2. Divide the mousse among 4 serving glasses. Chill for at least 1 hour before serving.

Tips: Garnish with fresh berries and a few chocolate shavings. The mousse can be stored in the refrigerator for up to 2 days.

Nutritional Info: Calories: 160 | Fat: 9g | Carbs: 20g | Protein: 3g[1]

PROTEIN CHIA SEED PUDDING

Prep: 5 mins | Cook: 0 mins | Serves: 4

INGREDIENTS:

- 400ml (1 2/3 cups) unsweetened almond milk
- 80g (1/2 cup) chia seeds
- 60ml (1/4 cup) honey
- 20g (2 tbsp) vanilla protein powder
- 5ml (1 tsp) vanilla extract

INSTRUCTIONS:

1. In a bowl, whisk together the almond milk, chia seeds, honey, protein powder, and vanilla extract. Let it sit for 5 minutes, then whisk again.
2. Divide the pudding among 4 serving glasses. Refrigerate for at least 2 hours or overnight.

Tips: Stir the pudding well before serving to ensure the chia seeds are evenly distributed. Top with fresh fruit or a sprinkle of granola.

Nutritional Info: Calories: 140 | Fat: 5g | Carbs: 20g | Protein: 5g[1]

PEANUT BUTTER BANANA BITES

Prep: 10 mins | Cook: 0 mins | Serves: 4

INGREDIENTS:

- 2 large bananas, peeled and sliced
- 60g (1/4 cup) natural peanut butter
- 30g (1/4 cup) granola
- 30g (1/4 cup) dark chocolate chips

INSTRUCTIONS:

1. Spread each banana slice with peanut butter and place on a parchmentlined tray.
2. Sprinkle the slices with granola and chocolate chips. Freeze for at least 2 hours before serving.

Tips: Use a fork to dip the banana slices in the peanut butter for easier handling. Store any leftovers in an airtight container in the freezer.

Nutritional Info: Calories: 160 | Fat: 7g | Carbs: 25g | Protein: 4g[1]

HEALTHY BROWNIES

Prep: 15 mins | Cook: 25 mins | Serves: 9

INGREDIENTS:

- 200g (1 1/4 cups) black beans, cooked and drained
- 75g (3/4 cup) unsweetened cocoa powder
- 120ml (1/2 cup) honey
- 60ml (1/4 cup) coconut oil, melted
- 5ml (1 tsp) vanilla extract

INSTRUCTIONS:

1. Preheat the oven to 180°C (350°F). Grease an 8inch square baking dish.
2. In a food processor, combine the black beans, cocoa powder, honey, coconut oil, and vanilla extract. Blend until smooth.
3. Spread the batter into the prepared dish. Bake for 25 minutes or until the edges start to pull away from the sides.

Tips: Let the brownies cool completely before cutting into squares. Store leftovers in the refrigerator for up to 5 days.

Nutritional Info: Calories: 120 | Fat: 5g | Carbs: 20g | Protein: 3g[1]

CARROT CAKE PROTEIN BARS

Prep: 15 mins | Cook: 25 mins | Serves: 9

INGREDIENTS:

- 150g (1 1/4 cups) wholemeal flour
- 30g (1/4 cup) vanilla protein powder
- 5ml (1 tsp) baking powder
- 5ml (1 tsp) ground cinnamon
- 60ml (1/4 cup) honey
- 120ml (1/2 cup) unsweetened applesauce
- 120g (1 cup) grated carrots
- 60g (1/2 cup) chopped walnuts

INSTRUCTIONS:

1. Preheat the oven to 180°C (350°F). Grease an 8inch square baking dish.
2. In a bowl, whisk together the flour, protein powder, baking powder, and cinnamon.
3. Stir in the honey, applesauce, carrots, and walnuts until well combined. Spread the batter into the prepared dish.
4. Bake for 25 minutes or until a toothpick inserted in the

center comes out clean.

Tips: For a sweeter bar, drizzle with a little honey after baking. These bars can be frozen for up to 3 months.

Nutritional Info: Calories: 130 | Fat: 4g | Carbs: 20g | Protein: 5g[1]

FROZEN YOGURT BARK

Prep: 10 mins | Cook: 0 mins | Serves: 4

INGREDIENTS:

- 500g (2 cups) lowfat Greek yogurt
- 60ml (1/4 cup) honey
- 80g (2/3 cup) mixed berries
- 30g (1/4 cup) granola

INSTRUCTIONS:

1. Line a baking sheet with parchment paper.
2. In a bowl, mix the yogurt and honey. Spread onto the prepared baking sheet.
3. Sprinkle with mixed berries and granola. Freeze for at least 2 hours or until firm.

Tips: Break the bark into pieces before serving. Store any leftovers in the freezer in an airtight container.

Nutritional Info: Calories: 110 | Fat: 2g | Carbs: 15g | Protein: 7g[1]

CHOCOLATE PIE SMOOTHIE

Prep: 5 mins | Cook: 0 mins | Serves: 2

INGREDIENTS:

- 240ml (1 cup) unsweetened almond milk
- 2 large bananas, peeled
- 30g (1/4 cup) unsweetened cocoa powder
- 60ml (1/4 cup) Greek yogurt
- 60ml (1/4 cup) honey

INSTRUCTIONS:

1. In a blender, combine the almond milk, bananas, cocoa powder, Greek yogurt, and honey. Blend until smooth.
2. Divide the smoothie between 2 glasses and serve immediately.

Tips: Add a handful of spinach for an extra nutrient boost. For a thicker smoothie, use frozen bananas.

Nutritional Info: Calories: 180 | Fat: 3g | Carbs: 35g | Protein: 6g[1]

BONUS: 28 day comprehensive meal plan for a DASH diet cookbook

Day 1

Breakfast: Berry Banana Overnight Oats

Lunch: Greek Salad, Minestrone Soup

Snack: Celery Sticks with Nut Butter

Dinner: Lemon Garlic Chicken, Roasted Vegetables

Dessert: Baked Apples

Day 2

Breakfast: Veggie Egg Frittata

Lunch: Chicken Fajita Salad, Broccoli Cheddar Soup

Snack: Frozen Grapes

Dinner: Cajun Salmon, Brown Rice, Green Beans

Dessert: Strawberry Shortcake

Day 3

Breakfast: Apple Cinnamon Overnight Oats

Lunch: Caprese Salad, Vegetable Lentil Soup

Snack: Carrots and Red Pepper Hummus

Dinner: Chicken Cacciatore, Quinoa, Roasted Brussels Sprouts

Dessert: Fruit Crumble

Day 4

Breakfast: Ham & Cheese Egg Cups

Lunch: Tuna Salad, Tomato Basil Soup

Snack: Apple Slices with Peanut Butter

Dinner: Veggie Fajitas

Dessert: Fruit and Yogurt Bars

Day 5

Breakfast: Pumpkin Spice Overnight Oats

Lunch: Chicken Caesar Salad, Italian Wedding Soup

Snack: Whole Grain Crackers and Cheese

Dinner: Chicken Tikka Masala

Dessert: Tropical Fruit Bowls

Day 6

Breakfast: Broccoli & Cheddar Egg Cups

Lunch: Strawberry Spinach Salad, Minestrone Soup

Snack: Fruit and Nut Trail Mix

Dinner: Shrimp and Veggie Kebabs

Dessert: Fruit Nachos

Day 7

Breakfast: Blueberry Muffin Overnight Oats

Lunch: Southwestern Quinoa Salad, Chicken Noodle Soup

Snack: Roasted Chickpeas

Dinner: Eggplant Parmesan

Dessert: Fruit Crepes

Day 8

Breakfast: Chocolate Cherry Overnight Oats

Lunch: Chicken Fajita Salad, Vegetarian Chili

Snack: Protein Balls 4 Ways

Dinner: Balsamic Chicken, Roasted Potatoes, Green Beans

Dessert: Fruit Pizza

Day 9

Breakfast: Carrot Cake Overnight Oats

Lunch: Greek Salad, Broccoli Cheddar Soup

Snack: Cucumber Tomato Salad

Dinner: Lentil Sloppy Joes

Dessert: Fruit and Yogurt Bars

Day 10

Breakfast: Apple Cinnamon Overnight Oats

Lunch: Caprese Salad, Italian Wedding Soup

Snack: Strawberries with Yogurt Dip

Dinner: Baked Cod, Brown Rice, Asparagus

Dessert: Mixed Berry Fruit Salad

Day 11

Breakfast: Spinach & Tomato Egg Cups

Lunch: Curried Chicken Salad, Minestrone Soup

Snack: Carrots and Red Pepper Hummus

Dinner: Buffalo Chicken Lettuce Wraps

Dessert: Baked Apples

Day 12

Breakfast: Blueberry Muffin Overnight Oats

Lunch: Tuna Salad, Vegetable Lentil Soup

Snack: Apple Slices with Peanut Butter

Dinner: Quinoa Stuffed Peppers

Dessert: Fruit Crumble

Day 13

Breakfast: Chocolate Peanut Butter Overnight Oats

Lunch: Cobb Salad, Tomato Basil Soup

Snack: Fruit and Nut Trail Mix

Dinner: Chicken Fried Rice

Dessert: Strawberry Shortcake

Day 14

Breakfast: Lemon Poppyseed Overnight Oats

Lunch: Avocado and Chickpea Salad, Chicken Noodle Soup

Snack: Roasted Chickpeas

Dinner: Orange Chicken, Brown Rice, Broccoli

Dessert: Tropical Fruit Bowls

Day 15

Breakfast: Berry Banana Overnight Oats

Lunch: Chicken Caesar Salad, Broccoli Cheddar Soup

Snack: Celery Sticks with Nut Butter

Dinner: Salmon Burgers, Sweet Potato Fries

Dessert: Fruit Crepes

Day 16

Breakfast: Sausage & Cheese Egg Cups

Lunch: Southwestern Quinoa Salad, Vegetarian Chili

Snack: Frozen Grapes

Dinner: Sweet Potato Black Bean Tacos

Dessert: Fruit Pizza

Day 17

Breakfast: Carrot Cake Overnight Oats

Lunch: Greek Salad, Italian Wedding Soup

Snack: Cucumber Tomato Salad

Dinner: Chicken Piccata, Angel Hair Pasta, Broccoli

Dessert: Fruit Nachos

Day 18

Breakfast: Blueberry Muffin Overnight Oats

Lunch: Chicken Fajita Salad, Minestrone Soup

Snack: Protein Balls 4 Ways

Dinner: Zucchini Lasagna

Dessert: Fruit and Yogurt Bars

Day 19

Breakfast: Strawberry Cheesecake Overnight Oats

Lunch: Caprese Salad, Vegetable Lentil Soup

Snack: Strawberries with Yogurt Dip

Dinner: Lemon Garlic Shrimp, Quinoa, Asparagus

Dessert: Mixed Berry Fruit Salad

Day 20

Breakfast: Chocolate Cherry Overnight Oats

Lunch: Tuna Salad, Tomato Basil Soup

Snack: Carrots and Red Pepper Hummus

Dinner: Portobello Mushroom Steaks

Dessert: Baked Apples

Day 21

Breakfast: Pumpkin Spice Overnight Oats

Lunch: Cobb Salad, Broccoli Cheddar Soup

Snack: Apple Slices with Peanut Butter

Dinner: Veggie Pot Pie

Dessert: Fruit Crumble

Day 22

Breakfast: Berry Banana Overnight Oats

Lunch: Chicken Caesar Salad, Italian Wedding Soup

Snack: Whole Grain Crackers and Cheese

Dinner: Baked Chicken Parmesan

Dessert: Strawberry Shortcake

Day 23

Breakfast: Veggie Egg Frittata

Lunch: Avocado and Chickpea Salad, Chicken Noodle Soup

Snack: Fruit and Nut Trail Mix

Dinner: Blackened Tilapia, Brown Rice, Green Beans

Dessert: Tropical Fruit Bowls

Day 24

Breakfast: Apple Cinnamon Overnight Oats

Lunch: Strawberry Spinach Salad, Vegetarian Chili

Snack: Roasted Chickpeas

Dinner: Broccoli Rice Casserole

Dessert: Fruit Crepes

Day 25

Breakfast: Blueberry Muffin Overnight Oats

Lunch: Curried Chicken Salad, Minestrone Soup

Snack: Celery Sticks with Nut Butter

Dinner: Chicken Piccata, Angel Hair Pasta, Broccoli

Dessert: Fruit Pizza

Day 26

Breakfast: Carrot Cake Overnight Oats

Lunch: Southwestern Quinoa Salad, Tomato Basil Soup

Snack: Frozen Grapes

Dinner: Coconut Shrimp, Brown Rice, Roasted Brussels Sprouts

Dessert: Fruit Nachos

Day 27

Breakfast: Chocolate Cherry Overnight Oats

Lunch: Tuna Salad, Broccoli Cheddar Soup

Snack: Protein Balls 4 Ways

Dinner: Chicken Fajitas

Dessert: Fruit and Yogurt Bars

Day 28

Breakfast: Berry Banana Overnight Oats

Lunch: Greek Salad, Vegetable Lentil Soup

Snack: Strawberries with Yogurt Dip

Dinner: Baked Cod, Quinoa, Asparagus

Dessert: Mixed Berry Fruit Salad

CONCLUSION

In conclusion, the DASH diet stands out as a scientifically-backed, sustainable approach to not only weight loss but also overall health and well-being. Understanding its principles, benefits, and practical strategies for implementation can significantly contribute to a healthier lifestyle. This dietary plan focuses on reducing sodium intake, promoting the consumption of nutrient-dense foods, and emphasizing a balanced approach to eating.

The scientific evidence supporting the DASH diet is robust, particularly in its positive impact on blood pressure and cardiovascular health. Compared to other popular diets, the DASH diet is distinctive for its emphasis on whole foods, especially fruits, vegetables, lean proteins, and whole grains. It goes beyond a mere focus on weight loss, targeting broader health aspects, making it a holistic approach to nutrition.

One of the key elements of the DASH diet is addressing the adverse effects of high sodium intake on blood pressure and overall health. Excessive sodium consumption has been linked to hypertension, a major risk factor for heart disease and stroke. The DASH diet's emphasis on reducing sodium intake can have profound health benefits, contributing to better blood pressure management and a reduced risk of cardiovascular diseases.

Furthermore, the correlation between reduced sodium intake and weight loss adds another layer of effectiveness to the DASH diet. By prioritizing whole, nutrient-dense foods and minimizing processed and high-sodium options, individuals following the DASH diet may naturally experience weight loss. This dual focus on both blood pressure management and weight loss sets the DASH diet apart from many other dietary approaches.

Implementing the DASH diet in daily life involves practical tips and strategies, especially when it comes to reducing sodium without sacrificing flavor. Specific food categories, such as snacks and main meals, can be adapted to align with DASH diet principles. The transition to a DASH diet lifestyle requires understanding its core principles, effective meal planning, and smart grocery shopping. Dining out can also be navigated successfully with the right knowledge and choices.

Overcoming common challenges associated with lifestyle changes is crucial for long-term success with the DASH diet. By addressing obstacles such as time constraints, taste preferences, and the availability of DASH-friendly options, individuals can make the diet a sustainable and enjoyable part of their lives.

The metabolism-boosting secrets associated with the DASH diet further contribute to its efficacy in weight loss. Understanding the role of metabolism in weight management and the science behind how the DASH diet affects metabolism provides valuable insights. With a focus on nutrient-dense foods and balanced meals, the DASH diet supports a healthy metabolism, fostering weight loss and overall well-being.

The comprehensive meal plans provided for breakfast, lunch, snacks, and dinner offer a diverse array of options that align with DASH diet principles. From overnight oats and egg dishes to salads, soups, and a variety of snacks, these recipes showcase the versatility and deliciousness of DASH-friendly meals. With a focus on lean proteins, whole grains, and abundant fruits and vegetables, these recipes cater to various taste preferences while adhering to the nutritional guidelines of the DASH diet.

In the realm of desserts, the DASH diet doesn't compromise on flavor or satisfaction. The inclusion of fruit-based desserts like mixed berry fruit salad and baked apples, alongside creative options like dark chocolate avocado mousse and protein chia seed pudding, adds a sweet touch to the DASH diet without sacrificing health goals.

In essence, the DASH diet offers a roadmap to a healthier, more balanced lifestyle. Its emphasis on reducing sodium, incorporating nutrient-dense foods, and supporting metabolism aligns with current scientific understanding of nutrition and wellness. The provided meal plans and recipes demonstrate that following the DASH diet doesn't mean sacrificing taste or variety. Instead, it opens the door to a world of delicious, satisfying, and health-promoting meals.

As individuals embark on their DASH diet journey, it's important to recognize that adopting any new dietary pattern takes time and adjustment. Consistency and commitment are key, and it's encouraging to know that the DASH diet not only contributes to weight loss but also offers a range of health benefits. Whether aiming to manage blood pressure, achieve weight loss, or enhance overall well-being, the DASH diet stands as a reliable and evidence-based choice in the realm of nutrition. By embracing its principles and incorporating the provided tips and recipes, individuals can embark on a journey towards a healthier, more balanced lifestyle with the DASH diet.

APPENDIX

Recipes Index

Printed in Great Britain
by Amazon

40650428R00071